LIFE IN TUDOR TIMES
A MASTER FILE
KEY STAGE 2

Editors

D C Perkins, BA (Hons), MEd, PhD (Wales) and E J Perkins, BSc (Hons), MEd

Illustration Anthony James

These Master Files are designed for use in the classroom. Each consists of teachers' notes, pupils' resource material, worksheets, activities and record sheet. Each book covers a part of the national curriculum in depth allowing the teacher to decide the amount of material to use according to the age and ability of the children.

DOMINO BOOKS (WALES) LTD
SWANSEA SA1 1 FN
Tel. 01792 459378   Fax. 01792 466337
www.dominobooks.co.uk   email: sales@dominobooks.co.uk

Life in Tudor Times Master File KS2 © EJP & DCP 1996
6th edition revised 2001, reprinted 2002
ISBN 1 85772 076 8

CONTENTS 1
TEACHERS' NOTES AND RESOURCES

Compiled by experienced teachers, **Life in Tudor Times Master File**, is a comprehensive coverage of the material needed for the National Curriculum at Key Stage 2. At this level, it is necessary to start from a chronological framework putting the Tudors firmly in the 16th century. Next, Children need to have a knowledge and understanding of Tudor attitudes and beliefs, the reasons why they acted in the ways they did. Events have to be named and explained and where there are different interpretations of the same event these should be given. Children must be encouraged to find out about Tudor history for themselves. To do this they need access to primary sources seeing, and if possible, examining copies of documents and artefacts. Visits to Tudor buildings and sites as well as museums concerned with 16th century times are essential. Children should learn to organise historical information and be able to communicate their knowledge through description and narrative. To cover the syllabus we shall deal with this study unit under the following headings.

	Page
LIFE IN TUDOR TIMES	4
Cross-curricular links and activities	4
TEACHERS' NOTES AND RESOURCES	5
How to use your Master File	5
The Tudors, a Brief History and Chronology	6
Houses of Lancaster and York	7
Tudor Monarchs Genealogical Table	8
Chronology of Events	9
A Tudor Time-Line of Events	9
Learning about the Past	12
Historical Sources	12
The Organisation of Government in Tudor Times	13
Pen Portraits of the Tudor Monarchs	14
Henry VII (1485 - 1509)	14
Henry VIII (1509 - 1547)	14
Edward VI (1547 - 1553)	15
Mary Tudor (1553 - 1558)	15
Elizabeth I (1558 - 1603)	16
[Mary Queen of Scots]	16
'Faction' and Life at Court in Tudor Times	17
The Rise and Fall of Thomas Wolsey	17
Local Government and How It was Organised	18
Tudor Society	18
Country Life in Tudor Times	19
A Tudor Village	20
Town Life in Tudor Times	22
London in the 16th century	21
The Reformation	25
Catholics and Protestants	25
The Dissolution of the Monasteries	26
Tudor Houses	27
Tudor Furniture and Fittings	27
Food and Drink	28
Education in Tudor Times	29
Schools	29
Universities	29

	Page
Tudor Clothes	30
Men	30
Women	30
Children	32
Sports and Pastimes	33
Sports and Pastimes	33
Music	34
Medicine and Health in Tudor Times	35
Medicine	35
Diseases	35
Health and Hygiene	36
The Tudor Poor	37
Poor Law	37
Crime and Punishment	38
The Tudor Navy	40
The Ships	40
Life at Sea	41
The *Mary Rose*	42
The Spanish Armada and its Defeat	43
The Course of the Spanish Armada	44
Women in Tudor Times	45
The English Renaissance	46
The New World and Voyages of Discovery	47
Tudor Personalities	48
Additional Teaching Ideas and Strategies	49
Visiting Historical Sites	51
The Importance of Visits	51
Preparation for a Site Visit	51
Teachers' Check List	52
Some Places to Visit	53
At the Site	54
Follow up to a Visit	54
Booklist and Resources	55
ANSWERS	101
RECORD SHEET	105

CONTENTS 2
PUPILS' RESOURCES/WORKSHEETS

	Page
TheTudor Monarchs Genealogical Table	56
I am King	57
Primary and Secondary Sources	58
School in Tudor Times	59
Henry VIII and his Six Wives	60
Closing the Monasteries	61
The Boy King - Edward VI	62
Mary Tudor - A Catholic Queen	63
The Nine Days' Queen	64
The Virgin Queen - Elizabeth I	65
The Death of a Queen	66
Tudor Apprentices	67
Work and Workers in Tudor Times	68
Life in a Tudor Village	69
How the Tudors Lived - a Cottage	70
How the Tudors Lived - A Manor House	71
How the Tudors Lived - A Mansion	72
Tudor Town Life	73
Tudor London	74
Tudor Eating Habits	75
A Tudor Dictionary Quiz	76
The Homeless in Tudor Times	77
Crime and Punishment	78
Tudor Dress - Men	79

	Page
Tudor Women	80
The Printing Press	81
The Boke of Husbandry, 1523	82
Medicine in Tudor Times	83
Sports and Pastimes	84
The Tudor Navy	85
The 'Mary Rose'	86
The Spanish Armada, 1588	87
Exploration in Tudor Times	88
Famous Tudors	89
Tudor Quiz	90
Tudor Objects	91
William Shakespeare	92
The Tudor Legacy	93
Tudor Documents	94
Letter from Queen Elizabeth I	94
Seals	94
Tudor Time-Line	95
Tudor Wordsearch	96
A Tudor Recipe	97
A Tudor Game	98
Project Ideas	99
Things to Make	99
World Map	100

THE TUDORS

CULTURE
The beginning of theatre
Books and printing
William Caxton
Poets
Playwrights
Shakespeare
England's Golden Age
Renaissance
Music

**THE MONARCHY
AND COURT LIFE**
Family trees
Tudor time-lines
Court life
The succession problems
Relations with France and
Spain
Privy Council
Star Chamber
The beginnings of
Parliament

**EXPLORATION
AND THE NAVY**
Famous journeys
Famous sailors
The New World
Conflicts with Spain
Beginnings of foreign trade
New trading companies
Naval growth
Admiralty
The *Mary Rose*
Spanish Armada

THE TUDORS
CROSS-CURRICULAR
LINKS
AND
ACTIVITIES

LAW
Tudor law
Crimes
Punishments
Poor law
Law and
superstition
Law
enforcements
JP's
Sheriffs
King's/Queen's
Law

RELIGION
Importance in
the Tudor period
Catholics
Protestants
Puritans
Heresy
England and the Pope
Reformation
Dissolution of the
Monasteries
Elizabeth's religious
settlement
The New Prayer Book
The Bible

**SOCIETY/
SOCIOLOGY**
Town and Country
The rich
The poor
Housing
Crime and punishment
Growth of the economy
The wool trade
New industries
Apprentices
Status of women
Husbandmen
Wives
Children
Merchants

ENGLISH
Cloze tests
Sequencing
Letters
Imaginative writing
Role play
Mime
Reporting
Speech making
Word searches
Word puzzles
Elizabethan English
Plays
Story telling

**MATHEMATICS
AND SCIENCE**
Time charts
Population changes
Price movements
Wages
Inflation
Printing Technology
Brick building
Glass making

MEDICINE
Medical
knowledge
Treatments
Physicians
Barber surgeons
Apothecaries
Sanitation
Heath care
Sweating sickness
The plague

TEACHERS' NOTES AND RESOURCES

HOW TO USE YOUR MASTER FILE

For many experienced teachers these few lines will seem superfluous. This book is planned to introduce pupils to the history of Britain. The degree of difficulty varies throughout the book. Following the National Curriculum guidelines, it is especially helpful for those between 7 - 11 years and it provides a background for older children as they proceed to more advanced work.

1. All the material in this book is photocopiable as defined on page 1. This means that all the material can be used in any way you wish in the classroom situation. Drawings may be photocopied and adapted for further work.

2. Covering sections of the master copies with plain paper enables resource material to be used in different ways. The questions may, if you wish, be omitted and you can use the drawings with your own questions.

3. Reduction of the A4 master copies to A5 means that they can be pasted in children's exercise books. The master copies can also be enlarged to A3 to make it easier for students to work on them as a group.

4. Some of your photocopies can be cut up to make additional puzzles and games.

5. It is intended that material be used at different levels depending on the ages and abilities of your pupils.

6. It may be possible to use some of the Teachers' Notes directly with more advanced and brighter students.

7. Some of the worksheets and resources are more difficult than others and the teacher has to decide the selection of appropriate material.

8. Some of the copy in the teachers' resources may be used in other ways, e.g. as cloze tests, sequencing exercises and so on.

9. Much of the completed work may be used as visual aids around the classroom.

10. Project work may be done individually, in groups and/or with teacher participation.

We hope you enjoy using this book and welcome any comments.

THE TUDORS
A BRIEF HISTORY AND CHRONOLOGY

The Tudors reigned for about a century and many changes occurred between the accession of the first Tudor, Henry VII, in 1485 (near the end of the 15th century) and the death of Elizabeth I in 1603 (at the beginning of the 17th century). At the outset explain to the children who the Tudors were: a family consisting of a line of kings and queens who ruled England for virtually the whole of the 16th century.

Next, it is necessary to establish where the Tudors come in the history of Britain.

ROMAN BRITAIN
55 BC TO AD 406

SAXONS AND VIKINGS
406 TO 1066

THE MIDDLE AGES
1066 TO 1485

THE TUDORS
1485 TO 1603

THE STUARTS
1603 TO 1714

THE GEORGIANS
1714 TO 1837

VICTORIAN BRITAIN
1837 TO 1901

MODERN BRITAIN
1901 TO THE PRESENT DAY

THE HOUSES OF LANCASTER AND YORK Explain how since the middle of the 15th century, two of the most powerful families in England - the Houses of Lancaster and York, both descendants of King Edward III - had been vying for the English throne. The Lancastrian symbol was a red rose and the Yorkist symbol was a white one. The Yorkists and Lancastrians fought over the succession and this civil war became known as the Wars of the Roses. Explain that the Tudor dynasty began after Henry Tudor (later Henry VII, Lancastrian, red rose) defeated Richard III (Yorkist, white rose) at the Battle of Bosworth Field in 1485. The white and red roses were combined to make the Tudor Rose (a double rose showing both families through Henry Tudor's marriage to Edward IV's daughter, Elizabeth of York).

The Tudor Rose

[Remember there were many other images and symbols connected with Tudor power and authority including
(a) the Royal coat of arms;
(b) the Royal monogram;
(c) the Royal titles e.g. *Defender of the Faith, In terra Supremu - Caput Ecclesie Anglicane* (on earth, Supreme Head of the Church of England) and
(d) the fleur-de-lys a symbol of French kingship used to signify England's claim to the throne of France].

The discussion about the Tudor Rose should lead to badges worn today: the children will have an assortment. What kind of badges do they wear? Do their families wear any? Have they noticed badges when they have been to particular places? Most will know about football badges and of course the school badge. Briefly discuss the importance of badges and what they signify: identification, belonging to a group - badges of rank, honour, scout and guide badges and so on. This will make the idea and importance of a Royal badge or emblem clearer. Remember, political parties have colours, emblems and badges. Discuss the history and development of such emblems and have the children design their own badges.

FAMILY TREES A good way of establishing the idea of chronology in young minds is for the children to produce their own genealogical table or family tree. This may be very simple beginning with great grandparents. Some children will be able to bring primary resource material to school such as drawings, photographs and birth certificates. They can use these to trace their ancestors. The following is a suggested format.

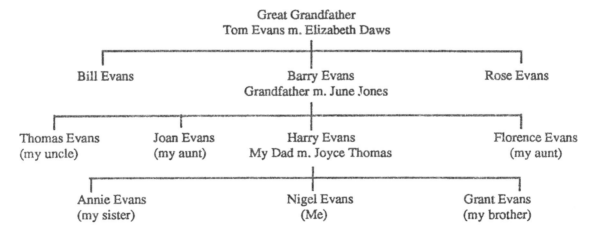

Then proceed to the Tudor table. (See next page). Remember to distinguish between the birth dates of monarchs and the dates they reigned. The table on the next page gives the reign dates.

Such family trees and chronologies make excellent material for use as resources for pupils later. Discuss family trees in general and make up a family for the children to practise on. Prepare cards showing the Tudor monarchs so that the children can see what they looked like. A time-line is important at this stage - make this general covering the whole period. You can consider specifics later when the children know more. Let the children also compile biographies of the Tudor monarchs. Small groups may produce biographies of different Tudors which are then brought together.

THE TUDOR MONARCHS
GENEALOGICAL TABLE

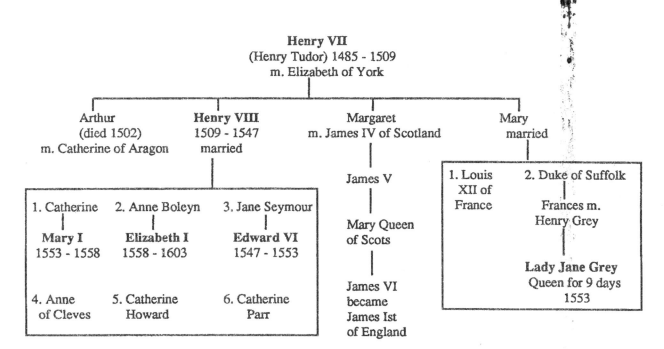

This chronology can also be shown in tabular form as follows.

NAME	DATES OF REIGN
Henry VII	1485 - 1509
Henry VIII	1509 - 1547
Edward VI	1547 - 1553
Mary I	1553 - 1558
Elizabeth I	1558 - 1603

CHRONOLOGY OF EVENTS

Introduce pupils to Tudor times by explaining that history pinpoints time by using such words as *age* or *period* and the name of a person/persons or event/s. The Tudors reigned from 1485 - 1603. Set the scene for the study by saying that during Tudor times, England was not a world power but a small country on the edge of Europe emerging from the Middle Ages. Much happened during the Tudor period and it can best be dealt with by using a topic approach. The main themes of study are examined in some detail in this book.

Time-lines are included where helpful and the children should be encouraged to produce their own in periods of ten years, i.e. time-line decades. They may produce such material using a computer. They may also be compiled under headings such as Housing, Education, Sports and Pastimes, Food and Diet, Law Enforcement, Medicine and so on. The children may add their own drawings and photographs to these. Such collections make attractive and informative displays and are usually well remembered. The time-line below covers most of the major events.

A TUDOR TIME-LINE OF EVENTS

1485	In August Henry Tudor defeated and killed Richard III at the Battle of Bosworth Field and became King Henry VII.
1486 - 7	Revolt of Lambert Simnel and the Earl of Lincoln suppressed.
1492	Henry VII's expedition to Boulogne. Treaty of Etaples.
1495 - 7	Perkin Warbeck's invasions of England.
1497	John Cabot sailed to Newfoundland.
1499	The execution of Perkin Warbeck and the Earl of Warwick.
1501	Arthur, Prince of Wales, married Catherine of Aragon.
1502	Arthur, Prince of Wales, died.
1509	Henry VII died. Accession of Henry VIII who married Catherine of Aragon.
1512	Wolsey became Henry VIII's chief minister.
1513	Henry VIII invaded France. The Earl of Surrey defeated and killed James IV of Scotland at the Battle of Flodden Field.
1514	Henry VIII's sister, Mary, married Louis XII of France. Wolsey began to build Hampton Court Palace and York Place (later Whitehall).
1516	Sir Thomas More's book, *Utopia* published. Henry VIII's daughter, Mary, was born.
1525	William Tyndale translated the New Testament into English. It was smuggled into England from the Netherlands.
1527	Henry VIII started divorce proceedings against Catherine of Aragon.
1529	Fall of Wolsey. The Reformation Parliament met.
1530	Wolsey died while being brought as a prisoner to London.
1531	Henry VIII separated from Catherine of Aragon.
1533	Henry VIII married Anne Boleyn who became Queen. Repudiation of Papal supremacy over the Church of England. Birth of Henry VIII's daughter, the future Elizabeth I. Thomas Cromwell became Henry VIII's chief minister.

1536	Anne Boleyn was executed. Henry VIII married Jane Seymour.
1536 - 9	Dissolution of the monasteries.
1536 - 7	Revolt of the Pilgrimage of Grace in Lincolnshire and Yorkshire.
1537	Edward VI born. Jane Seymour died. Henry VIII permitted the English translation of the Bible to be published.
1540	Henry VIII married and divorced Anne of Cleves. Fall and execution of Thomas Cromwell. Henry VIII married Catherine Howard.
1542	Catherine Howard executed.
1543	Henry VIII married Catherine Parr.
1545	France threatened to invade England. The royal vessel, the *Mary Rose* sank.
1547	Henry VIII died in January. Accession of Edward VI with the Duke of Somerset as Lord Protector. In February, Somerset and Archbishop Cranmer took the first steps to make England a Protestant nation.
1549	First Book of Common Prayer used in place of the Catholic Mass. Catholic revolt in Devon put down. Kett's agrarian revolt in Norfolk put down. In October, the Earl of Warwick (later Duke of Northumberland) overthrew Somerset.
1552	Somerset executed. The Second Book of Common Prayer introduced a more extreme form of Protestantism.
1533	In May, Willoughby and Chancellor sailed from London to find the North-East Passage.
1553	Edward VI died in July. Lady Jane Grey was proclaimed Queen. Mary Tudor defeated Jane Grey and became Queen. In August, Northumberland was executed and Protestant leaders arrested. Catholic Mass restored in December.
1554	In January, Sir Thomas Wyatt led a Protestant rebellion in Kent. In February, Wyatt's rebellion was defeated. Jane Grey was executed. Elizabeth was sent to the Tower. In July, Mary married Philip II of Spain who became King of England. In November, Cardinal Pole returned from exile and reunited England with Rome.
1555	The burning of Protestants began in February. Rogers and Hooper burned. In October, Ridley and Latimer were burned at Oxford.
1555 - 8	280 Protestants in all were burned.
1556	Cranmer burned at Oxford.
1558	In January, the French captured Calais. Mary died on November 17. Accession of Elizabeth I with William Cecil as Secretary of State.

1559	Elizabeth I rejected supremacy of the Pope and made England a Protestant nation once more. Third Book of Common Prayer published.
1560	On July 6, the Treaty of Edinburgh ended French control of Scotland. Scotland became a Protestant nation.
1561	Mary, Queen of Scots, returned from France to Scotland.
1563 - 4	17,000 died of the plague in London.
1566	Protestant revolt in the Netherlands against the rule of Philip II of Spain.
1567	Darnley murdered. Mary, Queen of Scots, deposed and imprisoned in Scotland. Protestants harshly repressed in the Netherlands by the Duke of Alva. Hawkins and Drake attacked by Spaniards in the West Indies. In December, Elizabeth I seized Alva's treasure-ships. Alva seized English property in the Netherlands.
1569 - 72	Hostility and economic sanctions between England and Spain.
1569	A Catholic rising in the North was suppressed by Elizabeth I.
1570	Pope Pius V's Bull excommunicated and deposed Elizabeth I.
1572	Massacre of Protestants by Catholics in Paris on St Bartholomew's Day. New outbreak of Protestant unrest in the Netherlands.
1576	First compulsory contribution imposed for alms for the impotent poor.
1576 - 8	Martin Frobisher's voyages to find the North-West Passage.
1577 - 80	Drake sailed round the world.
1584	Elizabeth I expelled the Spanish ambassador. Assassination of William the Silent by a Catholic in the Netherlands.
1585	Leicester led an army of English troops to help the Protestants in the Netherlands.
1585 - 6	Drake's expedition to the West Indies.
1586	The Babington plot. Trial of Mary, Queen of Scots, for treason.
1587	Execution of Mary, Queen of Scots. Drake attacked the Spanish Armada in Cadiz Harbour.
1588	Philip II planned to invade England. Defeat of the Spanish Armada.
1591	Sir Richard Grenville killed in sea-battle with Spaniards off the Azores. The Earl of Essex led English troops to help Henry IV against the Spaniards and Catholics in France.
1594 - 1603	Hugh O'Neill, Earl of Tyrone's, rebellion in Ireland.
1595	Sir Walter Raleigh's expedition to the River Orinoco in South America.
1595 - 6	Hawkins and Drake both died of disease while leading an expedition to the West Indies.
1596	An English expedition, under Essex, captured and burned Cadiz.

1597   New Poor Law legislation extended relief to the impotent poor (re-enacted in 1601).

1599   Essex's unsuccessful expedition to Ireland.

1601   Essex's rebellion: his defeat and execution.

1603   Elizabeth I died in March.
           Accession of James VI of Scotland as James I of England.
           38,000 people died of the plague in London.

LEARNING ABOUT THE PAST

Children need to know how historians find out about earlier times. Explain how a knowledge of the past comes from a variety of sources. When considering the Tudors include the following.

1. Archaeology. Many Tudor sites have been investigated and many buildings still remain intact. Note that Lavenham in Suffolk has survived largely unchanged and it shows us what a Tudor manufacturing town was like. Hampton Court, a Tudor palace, still stands. The raising of the *Mary Rose* is a more recent event and has given us insights into the Tudor navy and Tudor life. Note that a salvage team is contemplating the discovery and raising of Sir Frances Drake's coffin. Remember also that the Globe theatre has been reconstructed in Southwark, London and is now open.

2. Radioactive carbon dating.

3. Burial sites.

4. Sculpture and works of art many of which still remain.

5. Objects used by the Tudors which still survive - weapons, pottery, clothing such as armour, household items and bric à brac.

6. Tudor documents, writings and books. These include royal warrants and state papers e.g. Warrant to execute Mary Stuart, Queen of Scots, AD 1587. Other official and unofficial papers. Letters of important people e.g. Queen Elizabeth's letters. Diaries. The writings of travellers and visitors from other countries.

7. Tudor legal documents e.g deeds, assignments and wills. Building plans.

8. Writings of famous authors including plays, poems and other works e.g. Francis Bacon, William Shakespeare.

9. Paintings, drawings and carvings. Prints and woodcuts.

Whenever possible include such materials in the pupils' resources.

HISTORICAL SOURCES

Distinguish historical sources for the children. Explain how they are grouped into two types.

1. Original (or primary) Sources. These come from the time being studied such as a letter written by Queen Eizabeth.

2. Secondary Sources. These are books or materials about the past but written later. They are usually written by people who have studied the past (often from original sources).

Give the children exercises using original material if possible. There is a great deal available including Elizabeth's letters, accounts of visits to Tudor England by foreign ambassadors, original books like Stow's *Survey of London* and many Tudor woodcuts and prints. Pictures and passages from books are secondary work. Children need plenty of practice to enable them to distinguish between original and secondary material. Concentrate more on primary sources to help the children develop their critical awareness.

THE ORGANISATION OF GOVERNMENT

Although Parliament existed in the Tudor period, it is important to remember that it was the tool of the monarch. The real power was held by the King or Queen of the day. It was believed that the monarch held the position of power and authority through God's will. Later, this was given a name, rule by divine right. The monarch had the power of life and death over all the subjects of the realm. For ordinary people the head of state was, however, remote, residing in London and never seen by most people. Occasionally, monarchs stayed with important people in other parts of the country for 'a change' or to save money. People were not always pleased when they came to stay because it was a very expensive affair. The sovereign travelled with an extensive retinue.

Explain to the children the position of the Tudor monarchs and how they were all powerful. They ordered executions and rode roughshod over their people. The only one they felt responsible to was God. Draw a table for the children showing the position of the monarch and the subordinate positions of everyone else.

PARLIAMENT AND THE PRIVY COUNCIL IN TUDOR TIMES

During the Wars of the Roses, Parliament hardly met and it lost the confidence of the nation through its inactivity. Nevertheless, Henry VII encouraged it to serve his own purposes. First, he secured from Parliament confirmation of his title to the throne. Secondly, he used it to confirm the attainder of his enemies. Thirdly, he used it to confirm the confiscation of the take-over of the properties of rebels. Fourthly, he used it to get statutory authority for the Court of Star Chamber and lastly to confirm the judicial function exercised through his ministers, Empson and Dudley. By the middle of his reign Henry had succeeded in making himself wholly independent of Parliament financially and after 1497 he did not ask for any further grants. From then on he was able to rule without Parliament.

Explain to the children that Parliament at this time had little power. The monarch ruled and treated all opposition harshly. Emphasize that Henry VII made himself unassailable by using Parliament for his own ends. Once he was established, he almost ignored it.

The Tudor Coat of Arms

PEN PORTRAITS
OF THE TUDOR MONARCHS

It is important to give the children a brief resumé of the life and work of the Tudor monarchs. Do this in chronological order and spend most of the time on the two most important royals of the period: Henry VIII and his most successful daughter, Elizabeth I.

HENRY VII 1485 - 1509

Henry VII

Explain the importance of Henry VII in establishing the dynasty after a period of Civil War. The keyword is stability. Explain why he was shrewd to marry Elizabeth of York and so enhance his right to the English throne. Tell the stories of the people who wanted to take the throne from him - the Earl of Warwick and the pretenders, Lambert Simnel and Perkin Warbeck. The King showed further wisdom in money matters and the appointment of wise ministers like Edmund Dudley and Sir Richard Empson.

HENRY VIII 1509 - 1547

Henry VIII

Remember that this King was not expected to be the monarch and little is known about his early life. The death of his elder brother, Arthur, meant that Henry succeeded his father. He dominated English history in the first part of the 16th century. He was a true Renaissance prince - an agile athlete, a skilful knight, an accomplished scholar and musician - and with his bright auburn hair, a good looking, intelligent, energetic, young man: *the handsomest potentate in Europe* as one foreigner described him. It was Henry VIII who precipitated the English Reformation simply because he needed a son to succeed him.

Explain the terms 'Renaissance' and 'Reformation' and show how these movements were important in Henry VIII's day. Examine the dissolution of the religious houses and the causes and results of this. Show the contrasts between the young Henry and the King when he was old. Mention Thomas Wolsey, Bishop Fisher and Thomas More. Consider the changing attitudes to the Pope and Catholicism, to his first wife and to his other wives and show how he was motivated by the problem of the succession. It is important to remember also Henry's contributions to the navy and to education. Let the children do some research on these matters - a class project might be useful.

Consider the facts that Henry VIII
 (i) did little in the first half of his reign and a great deal in the second half;
 (ii) was easy going when a young man but became a tyrant later in his reign.
Explain why the King was always relatively popular and examine Henry's contribution to the demise of the Catholic Church in England and the onset of the Reformation. Remember that Henry VIII never ceased to be a Roman Catholic himself. Examine Henry VIII's relations with his contemporaries, his ministers and his wives. Consider the importance of court life in Henry VIII's time. Think of this monarch's reign as an exercise in extravagance and compare Henry VIII's lavishness with his father's parsimony.

Compare and contrast Henry VIII at the beginning of his life and at the end. A table might be useful.

YOUNG	OLD
1. Handsome	1. Grotesque
2. Slim	2. Fat
3. Good combatant, swordsman	3. Lost his earlier skills
4. Ambitious	4. Ambitious
5. Good horseman	5. Gave up riding or rode occasionally
6. Loved sport	6. Liked spectator sports
7. Extravagant	7. Extravagant
8. Supported the arts	8. Less interested in the arts

9. Fine musician	9. Became obsessed with the need for an heir
10. Eager to build up	10. Suffered illness -
(a) his reputation	(a) gout, followed by gangrene
(b) his navy	(b) syphilis
	(c) overweight. He had to be hoisted into bed or on to a horse
11. Very keen to establish the succession	11. Concerned with his personal safety and afraid to be alone. Feared assassination
12. Womaniser	12. Unscrupulous womaniser

Children always love a good story and whenever possible tell them one. The life and career of Thomas Wolsey is an example. Tell them what happened to Wolsey and how his life ended in ruins without the support of the King. This is a story with a very sad ending. Similarly, tell the story of the life of Henry VIII as one in which the King was always trying to make sure he left a secure throne to a male heir. Remember his throne eventually went to female children. Emphasize how a girl, Elizabeth I, was the most successful.

It is vital that you establish in the mind of your classes the factors which make up history. This is an examination of the causes and results of major events. The children must always examine 'why' things happened in the way they did. In Henry VIII's reign the causes and results of the Reformation and the Dissolution of the Monasteries are most important and we shall deal with these later in these notes.

EDWARD VI 1547 - 1553

Edward VI

Edward was the son of Henry VIII and Jane Seymour, his third wife. He was only 9 when he came to the throne and his reign lasted just six years. Protectors were appointed to look after state affairs. The first was his uncle, the Duke of Somerset, followed by the Duke of Northumberland.

Examine Somerset's and Northumberland's rule and the growth of Protestantism. The first English Prayer Book was published by Archbishop Cranmer in 1549, religious statues were barred and in 1552 Parliament passed an Act of Uniformity.

Before Edward died he was involved in a scheme to change the succession to the throne. He named 16 year old Lady Jane Grey, Henry VII's great granddaughter as his successor in an attempt to stop his Catholic sister, Mary, becoming Queen. The attempt failed, Jane was imprisoned and then beheaded. Mary became Queen.

Tell the story of the Nine Days' Queen and let the children re-tell it in their own words.

MARY I TUDOR (1553 - 1558)

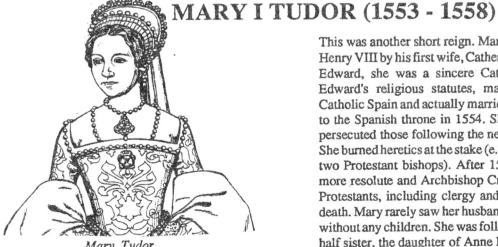

Mary Tudor

This was another short reign. Mary was the daughter of Henry VIII by his first wife, Catherine of Aragon. Unlike Edward, she was a sincere Catholic. She abolished Edward's religious statutes, made an alliance with Catholic Spain and actually married Prince Philip II heir to the Spanish throne in 1554. She was so devout she persecuted those following the new Protestant religion. She burned heretics at the stake (e.g. Latimer and Ridley, two Protestant bishops). After 1555 she became even more resolute and Archbishop Cranmer and some 280 Protestants, including clergy and laymen, were put to death. Mary rarely saw her husband and she died in 1558 without any children. She was followed by Elizabeth her half sister, the daughter of Anne Boleyn.

Examine Mary's reign and explain the attitude to religion - explain how religion at this time was more important than it is today. There were now good relations with Spain which changed dramatically in the next reign. Consider the reign of Mary from the point of view of being a Catholic and being a Protestant. The suffering of the Protestants needs to be emphasized. Pick one or two of the marytrs and tell the pathetic stories of their trials and deaths. Show how some people were brave and first tried to avoid death by renouncing

Protestantism. Discuss saints and sinners, martyrdom and trials. (Remember St Joan in the 14th century and how she died at the stake at Rouen.) If the children show interest, devise a 'mock' trial and get them involved in role play. Let them make a list of the most important martyrs.

ELIZABETH I (1558 - 1603)

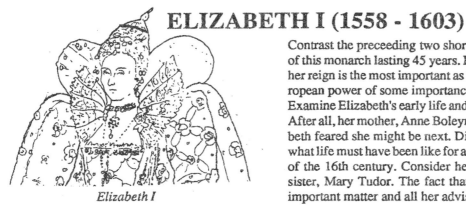

Elizabeth I

Contrast the preceeding two short reigns with the long one of this monarch lasting 45 years. From many points of view her reign is the most important as England emerges as a European power of some importance.

Examine Elizabeth's early life and her fear of an early death. After all, her mother, Anne Boleyn, was executed and Elizabeth feared she might be next. Discuss her upbringing and what life must have been like for a young royal in the middle of the 16th century. Consider her relations with her half-sister, Mary Tudor. The fact that she did not marry is an important matter and all her advisers wanted her to take a husband. Examine the implications of a marriage to Spain (Philip II), to a French king or to the Holy Roman Emperor. Show how she cleverly played off possible suitors against each other and how she used the fact that she was not married for political ends.

Elizabeth I's reign was full of intrigue and subterfuge - there were spies in this century as well as at other times. Show how she used this network to monitor events in this country and abroad. Cecil and Walsingham are important in this regard. Her tacit and eventually open support for the Protestant cause is important - the Netherlands are a good example and remember how reluctant she was to take action against Mary Queen of Scots but was eventually persuaded to sign her death warrant.

Foreign relations, especially with Spain, dominate the Elizabethan period. Consider the growth of the navy and the development of fighting ships and the growing capability to deal with the Spanish Armada. Remember that defeat of this Spanish invasion owed a great deal to luck as well as judgement. Give the children opportunities to discuss the causes and results of the Spanish Armada.

Examine the growth of English influence overseas, especially in the New World. The voyages of discovery were important as well as the prowess of English naval men. Explain how trade began to develop at this time and give some time to discussing manufactures especially in the wool trade.

Elizabeth's religious settlement was a compromise but look at this from the point of view of being a Catholic and being a Protestant at this time. Examine the laws, especially recusancy (fining people for not going to church). Religion was still very important and has to be examined in relation to political events.

This was when Renaissance learning was at its zenith. Remind the children about the growth of art and literature. Mention William Shakespeare and Francis Bacon. New inventions had helped to promote this new learning and consider the use of the printing press as a major development. Give an account of schools and education at this time and the position of children in Elizabeth's time.

Lastly, examine the problems of the succession at the death of Elizabeth. She was the Tudor Queen who ended the dynasty founded by her grandfather. In this event should she have married and secured the succession?

A good historical story is the lifeblood of history for young people. Look out for good stories and tell these to the children. A particularly 'good story' from this point of view is the colourful life of Mary Queen of Scots. Notes on her life are given below to remind you.

MARY QUEEN OF SCOTS

1. Mary was the daughter of James V of Scotland and Mary of Guise.
2. 1543 - 47 Proposed marriage between Mary Stuart and Edward VI failed because of the Battle of Pinkie Cleugh. Mary was sent to France.
3. Mary betrothed and married the Dauphin. He became King (1560). Died 1561 when Mary was only 19.
4. Mary returned to Scotland which was now Protestant and led by John Knox.
5. Mary married Darnley who was jealous of her secretary, Rizzio. Darnley had Rizzio murdered (1566).
6. Mary fell in love with Bothwell. Darnley mysteriously murdered at Kirk o'Field. Mary married Bothwell (1567).
7. Nobles rebelled. Battle of Carberry Hill. Mary was imprisoned at Loch Leven Castle but escaped.
8. New battle at Langside. Mary defeated and sought refuge in England.
9. Kept a virtual prisoner by Elizabeth. Centre of Catholic plots - Northern Earls', Ridolfi's, Throgmorton's and Babington's. Mary proved to be involved in the last plot. She was executed in 1587.

Show the children pictures and drawings of the Tudor monarchs so that they know what they looked like. This will get them firmly into their young minds.

'FACTION' AND LIFE AT COURT IN TUDOR TIMES

Throughout the Tudor period, government was largely organised through the Tudor court. The monarchs were despots who ruled with iron wills but used skilled administrators to help them. Under Henry VII and Henry VIII many of the leading government ministers were clergymen like Wolsey, Gardiner, Ruthall, Pace, Vannes and Edward Fox. The Tudors also began to use more common lawyers and laymen of comparatively low rank but with plenty of ability. Edmund Dudley was a simple Sussex gentleman and Richard Empson, a Northamptonshire squire. Men in high office had a whole range of secretaries and other officials to help them and it was these and the chief ministers who organised the government with the monarch's approval. Church influence faded as Elizabeth's time came near. Many of the secretaries in the reigns of Henry VIII and Edward VI were intellectuals like the poet, Thomas Wyatt, the Regius Professors of Civil Law and Greek, Thomas Smith and John Cheke, and the authors Thomas Elyot and William Thomas.

Secretaries and courtiers attached themselves throughout the period to an influential nobleman or minister at court under a system which was known as 'faction'. The favourite minister had his 'faction' and if he fell from power another faction was waiting to take over. It was a system by which the most powerful men engaged in a struggle for power and position with their subordinates supporting them because of personal affection, loyalty and self-interest. It was factions such as these that controlled Tudor government and this worked through the royal court and depended on royal patronage.

Life at court was not, of course, all intrigue for Tudor monarchs loved to enjoy themselves. It was a place for frivolity, for fun and games, for balls, pageants and masques, for music and laughter as well. The court was wherever the monarch was.

Life at court was elaborate and this became emphasized in Elizabeth's reign. Everyone was expected to kneel as the Queen passed by and no one spoke to her except on his or her knees unless the Queen gave permission for the person to get up. Only privileged officials whom she summoned were given access to the Privy Chamber and the Queen's private apartments. The appearance of Elizabeth at court was surrounded by much ceremony. This ceremonial side of court life was carefully maintained although there was no fixed place or residence for the court. It could be Whitehall, Hampton Court, Richmond or Greenwich. Elizabeth also visited other places. Wherever she was that was where the court was.

It is a good idea to make simple notes on the main ministers who worked for the Tudors. The brief notes below on Thomas Wolsley will give you the idea. These notes can then be used as a story-line for younger children e.g. **THE RISE AND FALL OF THOMAS WOLSEY**

Character
1. Intelligent, ambitious.
2. Liked ostentation, extravagance.
3. Hard worker, good administrator.
4. Rather immoral.
5. Dedicated to Henry VIII.

Career
1. Educated at Ipswich Grammar School and at Oxford - took a degree.
2. Entered the Church and became Dean of Lincoln and Chaplain to Henry VII.
3. Given state position as Royal Almoner, Director of Charities, Privy Councillor.
4. Arranged the Battle of Spurs and was rewarded by the Bishopric of Lincoln.
5. Offices showered on Wolsey. He became Bishop of Lincoln, Archbishop of York (1514), Cardinal (1515), Papal Legate and Lord Chancellor.
6. Controlled foreign and home policy from 1515 - 1529.
7. After 1525 he supported France and showed enmity to Spain, followed the policy of the Pope and not interested in maintaining the balance of power.
8. At home, he sold and distributed church and state offices, saw abuses in the church but did little to stop them. He helped to establish colleges at Ipswich and Oxford.
9. In 1529, Wolsey fell from power because he failed to negotiate Henry VIII's divorce.
10. Wolsey died in 1530 at Leicester Abbey.

The importance of the court in Tudor times needs attention. Describe this for the children and collect any paintings, drawings and similar material on court life. Read stories and collect pictures of Tudor court life. Get the children to imagine they are visitors to the court. Let them act as foreign ambassadors, envoys from foreign lands, even court jesters or players. Discuss how they would be received and treated. Concentrate on descriptions - food, entertainment, clothes, topics of conversation. Play Tudor music to provide an atmosphere. Get the children to suggest gifts they would give a Tudor monarch and suggest gifts they might have received. Let the children imagine they are nobles who have to invite the monarch to their mansion. Discuss how they would prepare for the visit and how they would entertain the monarch. Consider the cost.

LOCAL GOVERNMENT
AND HOW IT WAS ORGANISED

Local government in Tudor times was administered by the sheriff of the county, by mayors in towns and boroughs, by JPs in the shires, and by the parish bailiffs and constables and officers of the watch. The monarch appointed the sheriff who was usually the most prominent gentleman in his county. (After 1550 a Lord Lieutenant was appointed in each county with precedence over the sheriff.) The sheriff was responsible for arresting criminals and holding them in custody in the county jail. The general public were expected to catch fugitives from justice and JPs proclaimed a 'hue and cry' to find such criminals. From time to time the government adopted other methods of getting large numbers of the population to uphold the law. For example, an Act of Parliament was passed in 1534 which made everyone take an oath that he believed that the children of the King's marriage to Anne Boleyn would be the lawful heirs to the throne. Similarly, all holders of offices had to swear an Oath of Supremacy that Henry VIII was Head on Earth of the Church of England and a similar act was passed in Elizabeth's reign.

Despite the above, the system of law enforcement was haphazard but the law-abiding majority of English people ensured that, in general, order was maintained in nearly all the shires. At the beginning of the Tudor Age, there were two exceptions, Wales and parts of Northumberland. Eventually the Tudors enforced their authority over these areas as well.

TUDOR SOCIETY
THE UPPER AND LOWER CLASSES

Class and rank were very important in Tudor times. The first three groups made up the upper classes and the last two made up the lower classes. Those in the upper classes included courtiers, noblemen, bishops and senior abbots. The nobility had decreased greatly and it was Tudor policy not to increase their numbers for they were a powerful class who could challenge authority and take part in plots against the monarch.

ORGANISATION OF TUDOR SOCIETY

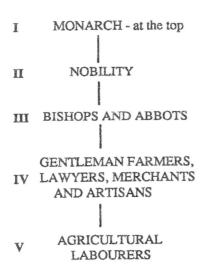

I   MONARCH - at the top

II   NOBILITY

III   BISHOPS AND ABBOTS

IV   GENTLEMAN FARMERS, LAWYERS, MERCHANTS AND ARTISANS

V   AGRICULTURAL LABOURERS

SOME REASONS FOR THE DECLINE OF THE NOBILITY

1. Many of them were old and died without heirs.
2. Many had been killed in the Wars of the Roses.
3. It was the monarch's policy not to create new peers.
4. Many nobles were not given high office and so their influence declined.
5. The early Tudors took titles away from those who opposed them.
6. Laws were passed against the nobility, e.g. the law that they were not to keep armed retainers.
7. Many were condemned to death for treason or traitorous conduct.

Indeed, at the beginning of Tudor times the lords spiritual appeared to be much more secure than the lords temporal. The bishops and abbots with seats in the House of Lords exceeded the number of nobles. There were two archbishops, nineteen bishops, twenty-eight abbots and two priors - 51 lords spiritual in all. There were 41 temporal peers - three dukes, one marquess, ten earls and twenty-seven barons. But even the ascendancy of the churchmen was shortlived because in 1536 and 1539, Henry VIII dissolved (closed) the major religious houses, confiscating their property and wealth. This diminished the power of the Catholic Church and increased his own wealth.

A new group emerged between the upper classes and lower classes. This was the middle class or middle men who held high offices in the prerogative of the monarch: gentleman farmers, lawyers, merchants and artisans. They worked for a living in the law courts, in trade and in manufacture. This class was to become more important later in the Tudor age as they became more influential and prosperous, and as townships grew. But the Tudor world was essentially an agricultural one and was more dependent on the land than anything

else. We must not forget the numerous members of the lower clergy in this analysis. In early Tudor times, the Church was the main avenue to advancement and priests were the educated men of Tudor society. Despite the steady decline of Roman Catholicism throughout the period the clergy were still important. Where the Catholics left a gap, it was filled by Protestant clergy.

The majority of people in Tudor times worked on the land. They were husbandmen who worked as agricultural labourers. There were numerous problems for the 16th century farmer which they and governement were trying to solve.

AGRICULTURAL PROBLEMS INCLUDED

1. A shortage of cheap, reliable labour.
2. Many people no longer wished to work on the land.
3. Farm workers (husbandmen) pressed for higher wages.
4. Farm workers pressed for shorter working hours.
5. Middlemen and 'regrators' bought foodstuffs cheaply and sold them at a high profit. This raised the cost of food and accelerated the need for better pay.
6. Rural housing was a problem.
7. The thriving wool trade meant farmers could make more money from raising sheep than growing crops.
8. The acreage of arable land decreased as pasture land increased.

Much about the work of farms and farmers in the 16th century can be learned from a best-seller of the period: *The Book of Husbandry* by Sir Anthony Fitzherbert or his brother John. Published in 1523, the book went to nine editions over a period of 45 years. The book was written for yeoman farmers, the self-employed who with their wives, managed farms and it gave advice on ploughing, sowing, lambing, repairs to the roads and animal diseases. One part of the book dealt in some detail with the role of the farmer's wife.

Finally, although serfdom was coming to an end (it had been abolished by statute in the 14th century) there were still some serfs in Tudor times and various Acts of Parliament created more throughout the century as a punishment.

Consider with the children the structure of Tudor society and the differences between life at the top (nobles) and life at the bottom (serfs). Let them consider the work of these people and the huge differences in the life styles between the wealthy and educated, and the poor and illiterate. Compare and contrast with society today. Let them write accounts of 'a day in the life' of particular Tudor people - a geat nobleman, a wealthy merchant, a gentleman farmer and an industrious but poor husbandman (farm worker). Consider the changes in these peoples' lives as the 16th century proceeded. Consider whether the changes were good or bad and how individuals were affected.

COUNTRY LIFE IN TUDOR TIMES

At the outset let us take a brief look at population figures. The figures below are estimated from tax and military service returns.

Date	Population (millions)
1066	2
1340	*4
1400	*2,100,000
1500	2,600,000
1600	4

The fall in the population between 1340 - 1400 was largely due to the plague (the Black Death) and other diseases.

In Tudor times, only about one fifth of the total population listed above lived in towns. The low-lying and fertile parts of the countryside was made up of large open fields, unbroken by hedges and only occasionally by stone boundary walls. Only in Devonshire and some parts of Kent were there small fields divided by hedges. Much of the countryside was wild and inhospitable. There were animals - deer, boar and wolves - roaming wild in parts of Wales and the North.

The countryside sometimes had roads, the King's highway, which linked the market towns. Where there were no market towns only rough tracks led to villages and farms. Most of the people travelling on the roads were on the way to or back from market. Most went on foot, some were on horseback while others drove a

flock of sheep or other animals. Carts were used to carry commodities especially foods such as fruit and vegetables.

A TUDOR VILLAGE

Life in the countryside centred on the village. Most Englishmen, and even more Englishwomen, never left the place where they were born, lived and died. Village life had changed little since medieval times with most people working on the land for the owner of a local manor. They might rent plots of ground from the local landowner to grow their own crops and there was 'common' land which was owned by all the villagers where they could feed their animals - cows, pigs, goats and poultry. This is how a typical village may have looked in Tudor times.

A Tudor Village

Note the watermill for sawing timber, the windmill for grinding flour, the manor where the local landowner lived, and the villagers' fields divided into strips and the enclosed fields with fences.

The typical village had several craftsmen - a wheelwright to make wheels, a carpenter to make and repair furniture, a smith to shoe horses and a weaver to make cloth and clothes. In many ways these villages were self-sufficient and in good years, people grew enough food to feed themselves. The only strangers they ever saw were wandering friars, pedlars selling goods and beggars of no fixed abode.

As time went on more and more open fields were enclosed to provide pastureland for sheep. This became a problem as land for 'common' grazing diminished and villagers found it hard to manage. Another growing problem was the shortage of wood. Wood was used to build ships, houses and furniture, was burnt for warmth and to make fuel for smiths' furnaces. Deforestation on a large scale alarmed the government and attempts were made to restrict tree-felling throughout the century.

The children need to have a grasp of Tudor class structure and the fact that England at this time was mainly agricultural. Towns were not important and life was centred in villages and farm communities. Paint a picture of life as a yeoman farmer or as an agricultural labourer for the children. Get them to play parts - role play - as a Nobleman, a bishop, an abbot, a lawyer, a merchant, an artisan, a priest, a gentleman farmer, an agricultural labourer, a serf ... Let them consider the position of women and girls in Tudor society and life in a village. Adapt the drawing above of a Tudor village and let the class make a Tudor village. This can be done with the whole class cutting out buildings and models or groups can work on the project. Also the children could adapt the society organisation ladder on page 18. They could draw people in Tudor society to illustrate a large version of this. Or they might prefer to make a collage showing society at this time. A collage can be expanded to include other occupations such as sailors, bowmen, abbots, priests and so on.

Let the children consider what it was like living in a Tudor village and compare and contrast life then with a typical English village today. Here are some of the differences.

TUDOR VILLAGE	VILLAGE TODAY
1. Isolated. No phones, no radio, no TV, few roads, no transport, no medical help.	Not isolated and linked into communication networks.
2. No regular water supply.	Regular, clean water supply.
3. No sanitation - no toilets or bathrooms.	Sewage and water systems. Toilets and bathrooms available.
4. No electricity.	Reliable electricity supply.
5. Villagers did not own their houses or land. High rents.	Many people own their own homes or rent at economic prices.
6. No waste or refuse collection.	Waste and refuse collections.
7. No post.	Good postal service.
8. No village shops or milk deliveries. Self sufficient.	Local shop/s and large shops easily reached. Not self sufficient.
9. No village school.	Education provided.
10. No help with disasters.	Help available when needed.
11. No news of events outside village.	Worldwide news available through newspapers, radio, TV, telephone, internet.

TOWN LIFE IN TUDOR TIMES

Towns in Tudor times, were in many ways overgrown villages. Even the larger towns had a 'rural aspect' and contained wide open spaces and open fields. The largest town was London with 50,000 inhabitants in 1500. Other towns and their populations are given below.

Town	Population in 1500
Norwich	13,000 people
Bristol	10,000
Newcastle	10,000
Salisbury	8,000
York	8,000
Exeter	8,000

Thirty other towns had a population of about 1,000 each.

Most towns were surrounded by their medieval walls. Within, the houses were mainly made of wood and built very close together. Towns at this time were unhealthy places. They had no proper drains or clean water. Human waste and rubbish were thrown into rivers or the streets. Horses, cattle, sheep, pigs and poultry added to the general filth. The only drinking water available was carried and sold by water-carriers. Wealthier people preferred to live outside the towns where the air was cleaner and there was more room to build.

Towns were already crowded, busy places where markets were held frequently selling produce brought in from the countryside. Cattle were brought into towns for slaughter in early Tudor times until finally, townspeople objected to the stench. Later, butchering was restricted. Sheep and pigs were driven into the towns on foot and kept alive. They wandered through the streets and into shops until they were slaughtered.

Townsmen usually walked everywhere but there were a few who could afford to own a horse. People who were ill or incapacitated sometimes travelled in litters carried by servants or drawn by horses: there were no coaches at the beginning of the Tudor period and even at the end there were few carriages. (Walter Rippon, a Dutchman built a carriage for Elizabeth I in 1564.)

Town streets were very narrow and were often paved with cobble-stones. There were no pavements. At night the streets were dark, lit by lanterns at corners or outside inns. Streets were dangerous places where thieves and footpads waited to attack citizens. Most people stayed inside their homes with well-bolted doors by dusk. When they had to go out they hired a 'link-boy' to light their way with a lantern or torch. Some towns had watchmen who patrolled the streets at night calling out the time each hour: 'One o'clock, a fine but cold night and all's well'.

During the day the streets were crowded, noisy and busy. Hawkers walked through them shouting about their wares. Tinkers, pedlars, basket-carriers, chair-menders, water carriers ... vied with each other to sell their goods and services and bartered with their customers. Carts and waggons rattled over the cobblestones.

In the larger towns all kinds of merchants traded: armourers, saddlers, goldsmiths, turners, coopers, fullers, dyers, masons, cutters, barbers, skin merchants, wool merchants and many more. The names of these tradesmen often became surnames. Thus, a man first known as Tom the Mason or Jack the Barber became Tom Mason and Jack Barber. Most merchants employed one or two boys learning their trade. These apprentices had a contract with their masters who agreed to feed, clothe and house them for seven years and teach them a trade. In return, a boy's parents paid a sum of money to the craftsman and the apprentice agreed to obey the rules of the trade and those set down by the town council. In some towns a curfew bell was rung each night at 9 o'clock by which time all apprentices had to be in the houses of their masters. Nevertheless, sometimes there were street fights between gangs of apprentices who were often unruly, attacking and robbing town dwellers.

Towns were centres of crafts and trade. Merchants and shopkeepers lived at their place of business. A shop which was in the front room of a typical house had a large window overlooking the streets. There was no glass but large wooden shutters which covered the windows at night. In the day, these were let down and used as counters. Behind the shops were merchants' offices or kitchens and above were the living rooms and bedrooms. Wealthy merchants had houses with three or four storeys and warehouses at the back. Houses by a river often had quays where cargoes could be unloaded direct from the ships. Merchants wrote letters with quill pens on stiff paper. There were no envelopes and the letters were sealed with hot wax which was marked with a ring, a seal, often bearing initials or a special design. There was no post and letters were sent by messenger.

The most serious dangers in towns were fire and disease. Most of the houses were built of wood and were close together. The situation did not improve until the end of the 17th century. Living so close together meant that any disease spread rapidly. Cholera and the plague were the worst and outbreaks occurred throughout the Tudor period. Smallpox and measles, new diseases at this time, killed many especially by the time of Elizabeth. Then there was the disease called the 'sweating sickness', similar to modern-day influenza. This started after 1485 and returned again and again especially in 1517, 1528 and 1551. In July 1517, 400 people died in Oxford in one week and in some towns up to half of the population died.

Towns were close to the countryside and most had fields where cows, pigs and sheep were reared. This proximity to the countryside had advantages and disadvantages. In later Tudor times, towns suffered from an influx of beggars, rural poor and others seeking work and refuge. Market scavengers were appointed to get rid of the begging poor. This was not so easy and workhouses were eventually opened for them. (See Elizabethan Poor Law Section.)

Finally, inns in towns became centres for social life. They were places where travelling merchants and local merchants met, where messengers and riders stopped en route for food and accommodation. News and information were exchanged. Games and pastimes developed at these inns such as bowls, cock-fighting, dicing and cards, while plays were performed in the inn yards - the birth of theatre.

Paint a picture in words for the children and discuss town life in Tudor times. Get the pupils to imagine a town with narrow streets, no pavements, full of litter and rubbish, wandering animals and vendors trying to sell their wares. What would it be like when it rained? What would life be like without electricity and street lights, without sanitation and running water? Compare and contrast life in a Tudor town with life in a town today.

Let the children pretend to be inhabitants of such a town or visitors to one - a pedlar, a street trader, a water carrier, a town crier, a rich merchant or a town misfit - a vagabond. There are many opportunities for role play. Draw, paint or make collages of people in a typical Tudor town. Make free-standing Tudor figures using papier maché and wire with wooden frames. Make models of town houses and let the children design posters to advertise goods they are selling.

LONDON IN THE 16TH CENTURY

In Tudor times, London was still essentially a medieval city. Although the population of 50,000 in 1500 was small compared with that of European capitals at that time (e.g. Paris 200,000), it was much bigger than any other town in England. The population grew rapidly to 100,000 by 1560 and to 200,000 by 1600. Even in the 16th century London was studded with fine buildings, royal palaces, civic halls and parish churches. The most impressive of these by the middle of Henry VIII's reign were the Tower of London, the King's residence of Baynard's Castle (built by his father in 1501), Bridewell Palace and York Place. The last-named had been built by Cardinal Wolsey, Henry VIII's chief minster, and when he fell from power in 1529 it became known as Whitehall. From then it became the chief residence of Henry VIII and his three children, Edward VI, Mary and Elizabeth I. Like all the large dwellings on the river in London and Westminster, it had private stairs leading down to the river and a landing place where residents could come and go by barge. Westminster Hall was about half a mile south of Whitehall. Here, important state meetings were held, the monarch addressed Parliament and the House of Lords sat. (The House of Commons met in St Stephen's Chapel which was

adjacent.) Westminster Hall was also the venue for the King's common law court, the Court of King's Bench and the place where great state trials were held. It was also used for coronation banquets after the crowning ceremony at nearby Westminster Abbey. The Abbey was one of the most important of the 313 monasteries in England and the richest with an annual income of £2,409.

John Stow was a Londoner, born in 1525. Son of a tallow chandler of Throgmorton Street, he became a merchant tailor. He lived all his life in the City inside Aldgate. He wrote an important book on London in Tudor times called, *Survey of London*. Published in 1598, this described the buildings and life in the City. It gives a fascinating picture of life in the 16th century. From this book we learn that London may be regarded as having three parts. First, there was the City at the centre, the commercial and industrial dynamo, densely populated, prosperous and busy. Added to the many churches and Company Halls was the new Royal Exchange founded by Thomas Gresham, the Elizabethan financier, in 1571. Here rich and poor, alderman and commoner lived together in a conglomeration of streets, alleys and courts. Secondly, the area to the west of the City stretching along the Strand to Westminster. This was a developing area. Here the landed gentry, government servants and lawyers, professional and political people lived in stately houses on the Thames bank or in the legal quarter around Fleet Street.

The third area to the north and east, (in Southwark and its surroundings) was mainly occupied by craftsmen and semi-skilled workers. There were few housing amenities but the workforce grew rapidly and was augmented by shipwrights and sailors who later formed the basis of a thriving overseas business. London's status as Britain's largest port was laid down in the 16th century. By 1600 ships were setting sail from Deptford, Wapping and Ratcliffe for countries abroad. Companies of merchants were founded which helped British trade, for example, the East India company (founded 1600). Several company halls, the headquarters of the guilds and livery companies began. Each had its own distinctive badge or shield.

 Mercers

 Grocers

 Drapers

 Fishmongers

Goldsmiths

 Skinners

 Merchant Taylors

 Haberdashers

 Vintners

 Clothworkers

In Tudor times the only routes into London by land were through the gates in the City wall which were closed at nightfall. There were ten gates around the City. London Bridge was the only one across the Thames between the sea and the crossing at Kingston more than twenty miles up river. Most of the bridge was made of stone except for the southern end where there was a wooden drawbridge. It was customary to put the heads of executed people on poles on Bridgegate on London Bridge as a warning to those entering the City.

London's water supply was poor. There were good supplies outside the City at places like Clerkenwell and Sadler's Well. Inside, most people fetched their water from two streams which flowed through the middle of the City into the Thames. These were the Fleet Ditch or the Walbrook. Carriers were employed to carry water in buckets which they hung from a yolk across their shoulders or in large tankards like milk churns.

Paint a picture of London at this time in words and describe what it must have been like to live there. Show what large buildings there are in the City today and note some that were built in Tudor times. Tell the children about the great guilds of livery companies that began at this time. Let the children colour their shields as part of their work. Pinpoint the difficulties of getting into London and crossing the Thames. Illustrate from maps and diagrams how small London was in Tudor times. Emphasize how little of the metropolis had been built and consider the city south of the Thames - virtually still country areas. Discuss the differences between London in 1500 and in 1600. Use extracts from Stow's work for exercises on Tudor London. Discuss why so many Londoners used visual material at this time to attract their customers. Compare and contrast London then with London today.

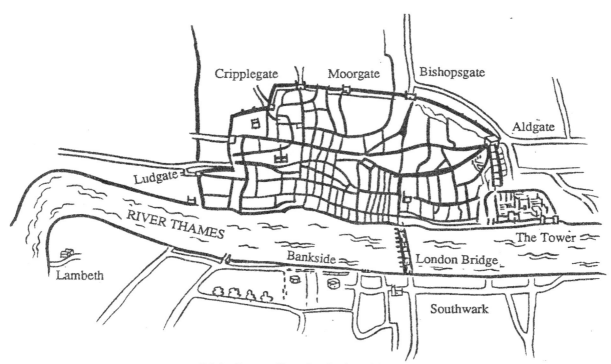

Main Gates of London in the 16th century

London Bridge showing Bridgegate with its row of heads stuck on poles

London Bridge was a 'living' bridge (that is people lived and worked on it). At the moment there are no living bridges but plans to build one across the Thames are being discussed.

THE REFORMATION
CATHOLICS AND PROTESTANTS

At the outset, children need to be told how important religion was in the 16th century. The major religion in Europe was Roman Catholicism. The head of the Roman Catholic Church was the Pope who lived at its centre or headquarters in Rome. The papacy has a long history stretching back to the beginnings of the Christian faith. The Pope was Christ's representative on earth and spent his time (or he was supposed to) converting unbelievers to the faith. [The Society of Jesus (The Jesuits) were important in this endeavour later.]

The people of England had been staunch Roman Catholics for centuries. English Kings had gone abroad in the past to fight for the faith against the infidel: these early battles were called the Crusades. Explain the meaning of a Crusade and when they took place. Explain that England was a Catholic country at the beginning of the Tudor period.

In the 16th century people began to examine the Church critically for the first time. Martin Luther's work is important in this regard. Tell the story of Martin Luther and what he did. Explain Henry's VIII's reaction for which he was made 'Defender of the Faith'.

History, as we have noted earlier, concerns causes and effects. We should examine the reasons for historical events and the results.

THE REASONS FOR THE REFORMATION IN ENGLAND include.
1. The need for Henry VIII to divorce Catherine of Aragon and marry Anne Boleyn - she was the immediate cause.
2. The need for Henry VIII to leave a secure throne. He needed a male heir.
3. The reluctance of the Pope to grant Henry VIII a divorce.
4. The state of the Church. There were many abuses and some clergy were regarded as too worldly.
5. The examples of reformers abroad, e.g. Martin Luther.
6. The riches of the Church were there for the taking. Note the Dissolution of the Monasteries 1536/1539.

Tell the children the story of the break-up of Henry VIII's marriage and also tell them the story from Catherine of Aragon's point of view - she was a good wife, a good mother, a fine queen, a religious person, proud and a true Spanish princess. Remember that Henry VIII did not really want to become Protestant and he remained in reality a Catholic king. But he would not brook any interference with his authority and so he carried through the 'reform' (the reformation) to its bitter end. The results of the reformation were more far reaching than he ever imagined.

RESULTS
1. England became a Protestant nation.
2. The Church of England began.
3. The monarch became the head of the Church of England.
4. England became a target for the Catholic nations - France and Spain.
5. Church lands began to disappear with the Dissolution of the Monasteries.
6. The King became richer and gave many of the Church lands to his supporters.
7. There was no turning back. Mary Tudor tried to turn the clock back but was unsuccessful.
8. In Elizabeth's reign the monarch became the champion of Protestant causes, e.g. in the Netherlands.
9. New groups began to appear - the staunch Protestants and the Puritans.
10. People began to fear Roman Catholics - their intrigues and revolts.

Children do not always realise that religion can be as important to people as it was in the 16th century. Now we have freedom of religion, then people died for their beliefs. Make sure that they know the meanings of terms such as Catholic, Protestant, Puritan, Reformation and Dissolution of the Monasteries. Explain that people were willing to die for their faith and be sure thay understand the meaning of martyr. Tell stories about some who died at the stake. Draw pictures and let the children write about famous Catholics and Protestants. Remember Archbishop Cranmer and Bishops Ridley and Latimer. Outline the causes and results of church reform.

THE DISSOLUTION
OF THE MONASTERIES

This was the final nail in the Reformation coffin. Once again it is important to emphasize the causes and results. The effects on ordinary peoples' lives are another consideration. Remember that at the beginning of the Tudor period the 513 monasteries and 130 nunneries were in no danger of suppression. Remember too, that the Act of Union between England and Wales meant that the Principality was also involved.

This is a good time to introduce the children to the life and work of a monastery. Tell them about the dedication to prayer - monks attended mass eight times a day and spent their lives in study and contemplation. The monasteries employed many people and they supervised the work of servants and labourers in the fields. Many monks taught locally and some were given dispensation to lecture at Oxford and Cambridge Universities. Pinpoint the reasons for the Dissolution.

REASONS FOR THE DISSOLUTION

1. Many monks had acquired a bad reputation. some were immoral and investigators pinpointed the vices of monks and nuns.
2. Monasteries owned land and were wealthy. Monks were often unpopular with their tenants.
   Many were harsh and greedy landlords. They had become too wealthy.
3. Henry VIII wanted to take over the wealth of the monasteries.
4. The King wanted to complete the break with Rome.
5. The King wanted to complete the centralisation of power in his own hands.
6. The monasteries had many enemies.
7. Monasteries no longer useful - truer of the South than of the North.
8. It was a way of securing the permanence of the Reformation, created a vested interest - the new landowner.
9. Examples from the Continent. Luther and Zwingli had dissolved monasteries.
10. One of the most important reasons - the monasteries were centres of unrest and possible plots from the Catholics and Rome would come through them.

In 1536 the smaller monasteries with an annual income of less than £200 were closed. The others were closed in 1539. The results were important economically and socially.

RESULTS

1. Monks were paid pensions by the royal treasury for the rest of their lives. The sums varied from £100 a year for an abbot to £5 a year for a monk.
2. Many monks joined the ranks of the unemployed.
3. Thousands of servants and labourers got nothing. They added to the number of vagabonds who existed in Tudor times. Chapeys, the Holy Roman Emperor's ambassador reported that 20,000 former inmates of the monasteries were begging on the streets but this was probably an exaggeration.
4. The King became wealthier. He pocketed the revenue he received for some monastic lands.
5. The separation from Rome was complete.
6. The King could reward his faithful servants with monastery lands and buildings. This created a vested interest in the dissolution: a group who wanted to keep the church property they had acquired.
7. Education suffered because many monks who had been teachers were no longer available.
8. Riots in many areas where people depended on the monasteries for their living.
9. The Pilgrimage of Grace rebellion was a direct result of the dissolution of Hexham Abbey in Northumbria.
10. The new landowners enclosed land and extensively converted arable land into pasture. There was less land for common use.
11. The woollen industry received a considerable stimulus from the land now available for sheep pasture.
12. The political and social and economic influence of London, in particular, increased. The City acquired from the Crown many rights that had been held by the monasteries and much ecclesiastical property that could be used for residential and business purposes. This helped the City to grow and develop.

This historical event provides excellent material for role play for the children. Some of the roles could be:

1. Investigator visiting a monastery.
2. Investigation of the abbot of a monastery.
3. Inspector taking an inventory of monastery lands, goods and chattels.
4. Local reporter investigating the local problems caused by the closure of a monastery.
5. A labourer who used to work on monastery land reporting his problems because he has lost his job.

Let the children pretend to be monks. They can bring their dressing gowns. Let them hear a recording of a Latin prayer, read it and explain it. If possible visit an abbey or monastery. A derelict or closed one is still useful. Point out the buildings where the monks lived and worked - the solitary cells, the monks' walk, the place where they held religious services. Let the children investigate what happened to some of the monasteries, abbeys or nunneries. A local one can provide much material for a class project.

TUDOR HOUSES
FURNITURE AND FITTINGS, FOOD AND DRINK

TUDOR HOUSES

In the Middle Ages, poor people, husbandmen and labourers lived in small, one-roomed cottages made of wood. Their situation had changed little by Tudor times although a bedroom or two might have been added in the roof reached by a ladder. Many country cottages newly built in the early 16th century had wooden frames pinned together with wooden pegs with the spaces filled with clay or brick. Some were made a little more comfortable and warmer because instead of holes in the roof for the smoke from the fire to escape, they had a proper chimney. This also prevented thatched roofs catching fire. The chimney was half timbered and there was no glass in the windows. (See worksheets for drawing.)

Up and coming tradesmen, farmers and artisans wanted to live in better circumstances. In the 16th century they began to build houses with a private room (a solar), a parlour and a few additional rooms. Some of these better houses often had small glass windows. More prosperous country gentlemen began to build larger dwellings. These were Tudor manor houses. They had separate rooms for dining and sleeping, staircases and glass windows. They had tiled roofs and tall chimneys. (See worksheets for drawing.)

But as late as 1598, most people still lived in small houses made of wood with two storeys. Most houses were put up by local men who were very poor craftsmen.

Nobles, who held high positions in church and state often built magnificent houses in town and countryside. This prestige building was carried out by new entrepreneurs, businessmen who employed scores of workmen who worked all over the country on building contracts. They built in brick and stone. Some began to earn reputations for themselves. Wastell built the tower of Canterbury Cathedral, Henry VIII's chapel in Westminster and chapels in Peterborough Cathedral and King's College, Cambridge. William Virtue worked on St George's Chapel and the Lady Chapel at Windsor, King's College, Cambridge, on Corpus Christi College, Oxford and on the chapel of St Peter and Vincula in the Tower of London. Henry Redman carried out work at Eton, Greenwich, Windsor Castle and built Hampton Court Palace and York Place for Thomas Wolsey. Some of the superior palaces and houses built at this time include Woburn Abbey, Wilton Abbey, Beakesbourne Palace, Kirby Hall, Wollaton and Longleat House.

Features of these huge mansions included a large dining room, a set of state apartments and a long gallery. The long gallery was regarded as most important because it could be used for entertaining, for music and dancing, for games and as an exercise area when the weather outside was bad. The hall was often used as a living room and a dining hall for the family and servants. As glass became more readily available and cheaper, Tudor builders used much more of it. These larger houses also had big, formal gardens with paths and flower beds and low hedges at the side. Taller hedges were often clipped into animal shapes. Ornate and complicated mazes were also popular features.

TUDOR FURNITURE AND FITTINGS

In Tudor times ordinary Englishmen were still using furniture typical of the Middle Ages. Husbandmen had a few simple wooden stools, one or two wooden chairs, a wooden table, a wooden bed and perhaps a wooden chest.

The King, the nobility and the wealthy depended mainly on the mighty oak. Solid oak chairs, tables, chests and beds were elaborately carved and there were ornate open cupboards, where plate and silver were displayed. Household linen and clothes were kept in carved oak chests which also served as places to sit. From 1550 Flemish craftsmen were employed and they improved the quality of the design of furniture but it was not until near the end of the period (1600) that the first upholstered furniture and the first chest of drawers appeared. But even before this the Tudors had used elaborate cushions on furniture and the floor. Wealthy families had large four poster beds surrounded by curtains. Poorer families had large beds (without the curtains) where servants and labourers slept together.

The walls of rooms in ordinary houses were made of plaster whilst the wealthy used finely carved oak panelling. There were few pictures and instead wealthier folk hung tapestries on the walls. (biblical scenes were popular). There were few carpets and most people depended on loose rushes or woven rush mats.

Ironware was a favourite with the wealthy, usually iron chests, iron lampholders, iron fire-dogs and firebacks.

FOOD AND DRINK

The eating utensils of ordinary families were very simple. The poor ate from trenchers made from pieces of stale bread or wood (wooden plates). There was no table cloth. The father and mother sat on stools whilst the children ate standing up. Soup and porridge were eaten from bowls called 'porringers', fruit and sweets were served on special dishes called 'roundels'. Yeoman farmers and merchants used pewter plates. Every household had at least one knife (made in Sheffield, Yorkshire since the 14th century) but there were no forks. All classes cut up their meat with a knife and popped it into their mouths with their fingers. Spoons were readily available and were used for soups and other dishes. Poorer families had wooden spoons and yeomen tended to use those made of pewter. Goblets for these classes were also made of wood and pewter. The wealthy ate from gold and silver plates, had knives and spoons made of silver as well as silver and gold goblets.

In the 16th century ordinary people got up at 5 am in the summer and 6 am in the winter. The working day was governed by the hours of daylight. After attending prayers, they had breakfast by 6.45 am and then they set about their work. At about 11 am they ate their main meal, their dinner, then they carried on working until 5 or 6 pm. Artisans usually continued until 7 pm. They then had supper and went to bed at 9 pm.

Husbandmen and poor farmers had roast meat only once or twice a week. On other days they had to be satisfied with pease or pottage (a kind of soup) with a lump of bacon or pork in it, fish, eggs, butter and churned milk. They also had cider, beer or ale. (Ale was dearer than beer.) Town dwellers usually had more meat than these country folk including brawn, bacon, beef, mutton, capons and pigeons. Most people ate fresh or salted fish on Fridays and during Lent. Most ate coarse brown bread made from rye or barley or, in times of scarcity, from acorns. Only the well-off ate white bread made from wheat. The Tudors ate better than their contemporaries in Europe.

In the mansions of the nobility, gentlemen and the rich merchants, dinner was regarded as an important occasion especially if there were guests. The table was covered by a fine linen cloth, each place laid with a plate, a napkin, knife, spoon and wine goblet. All diners were seated and waited upon by servants. As well there would be an aquamanile or ewer used to pour water over sticky fingers. The meal could last for two to three hours and there was a wide choice of dishes. These people drank home-made ale and beer or wine imported from France. Wine was kept cool in a tub of water. Each time a guest wanted a drink, the glass was rinsed in a wooden tub before it was refilled. The English were fond of sweet foods and honey was used because sugar was so expensive.

The very wealthy including the monarch had huge banquets. They often sat at table for seven hours or more. They drank expensive wines from France, Malmsey from Greece and dearest of all, hypocras, a liquer from Smyrna and the Levant. The following is an account of a dinner given by the Marquis of Exeter for Henry VIII in 1533.

First Course:
Salads of damson, artichokes, cabbage lettuces, purslane and cucumber with which were served cold dishes of stew-sparrow, carp, capons in lemon, larded pheasant, duck, gulls, brews, stuffed rabbit, pasty of venison from fallow deer and pear pasty.

Second Course:
Served hot, stork, gannet, heron, pullets, quail, partridge, fresh sturgeon, pasty of venison from red deer, chickens baked in caudle and fritters.

Third Course:
Jelly, blancmange, apple with pistachios, pears with caraway, filberts, scraped cheese with sugar, clotted cream with sugar, quince pie, marchpane, wafers and spiced wine.

Discuss Tudor eating habits with the children and what people ate at that time. Explain how they ate with their fingers. The children should be able to understand why diet was considered important in medical circles especially if they consider the food of the wealthy. (See Section on Medicine.) Discuss typical meals for the poor, the not so poor and the wealthy. Show how new foods e.g. potatoes and sugar arrived in this century and discuss the problems of keeping food fresh. Examine feasting and fasting at this time. Compare and contrast Tudor food with food today.

EDUCATION IN TUDOR TIMES
SCHOOLS

The kind of school a child attended depended on the class of his or her parents. Education tended to widen the divide between the classes. In some areas children were not educated at all. Most children, the sons and daughters of agricultural workers, depended on local parish schools for any education they received. The parish priest taught the alphabet, simple arithmetic and enough Latin for children to learn the Lord's Prayer, the Ave and the Creed. Formal education for these lower classes was haphazard to say the least.

The principal provider of education elsewhere for the children of better off families, the sons of gentlemen, was the Roman Catholic Church. These children went to the grammar schools that existed throughout the country attached to monasteries, abbeys, churches and cathedrals. There were very few independent schools: Winchester had been founded in the 14th century (1387) and Eton College in the 15th (1440). Harrow was founded in Tudor times by the yeoman, John Lyon.

The sons of the upper classes did not attend such schools. The nobles educated their sons at home and employed personal tutors.

Those who received a formal education spent a long time at school. After three years at a 'petty' (nursery) school they started at the grammar school at the age of seven. They were first taught the trivium, the three subjects grammar, dialectic(logic) and rhetoric (the effective use of language). Later, they advanced to the quadrivium which included geometry, arithmetic, music and astronomy. In many respects this education was quite wide for it included English grammar, composition in Latin in verse and prose, elementary ancient history, geography, simple arithmetic, the elements of the church calendar, the philosophy of Aristotle, St Augustine, Anselm and Thomas Aquinas, the plainsong rules of church music, the theory of the harmony of numbers, the current theories about the medical properties of plants and foods and the movements of the celestial bodies (a mixture of astronomy and astrology). They learnt no science or French although the sons of the monarch learned to speak and write French fluently.

The school day began early in the morning at 7 am, lunch was at 11 o'clock and afternoon lessons lasted from 1 pm to 5 pm. No time was allotted for play or physical recreation. In early Tudor times before the dissemination of the printed word, horn books were used in schools. A horn book consisted of a wooden board with a handle and pieces of paper stuck on the wood. Text such as the alphabet or Lord's Prayer might be written on the paper which was covered with a thin layer of horn to protect it. The text usually started with the sign of the cross and the books were sometimes called criss-cross books.

Discipline was harsh and boys who forgot their lessons were flogged.

Girls were taught at separate schools attached to monasteries and nunneries. After the invention of the printing press books were more readily available and girls as well as boys were taught to read and write. Teachers at all the schools were male.

UNIVERSITIES

A few grammar school boys went on to the two universities that existed at this time, Oxford and Cambridge both founded in the 13th century. Boys normally attended at the age of 14 but exceptional pupils were admitted even earlier, e.g. Thomas Wolsey was admitted at the age of 11. Here they studied Latin, canon law, Roman civil law and medicine. Later in the Tudor period Greek became an important subject because of the influence of the Renaissance. (The common law of England was taught only in the four Inns of Court in London.) Women were not admitted to the universities.

Education suffered greatly when the monasteries closed and many grammar schools disappeared altogether. Boys from poorer familes tended to learn a trade such as carpentry or cloth making instead of going to school. They were indentured as apprentices for seven years. Girls stayed at home and learned to sew, cook and run the household.

The children should know about schools in Tudor times and how they differed from schools today. Compare and contrast the subjects taught. Discuss the merits of schools without science and without any fixed time for recreation and play. Discuss the length of the school day (taking up most of the daylight hours). Consider the problems faced by children and schoolteachers in the 16th century. Discuss the pros and cons of separate education for boys and girls and the system today of educating everyone together.

Let the children write or act an account of a day in the life of a Tudor schoolchild. Let the children make a hornbook out of stiff cardboard. They could write the text on a piece of paper and paste it on the board then cover it with transparent film or sellotape instead of horn.

TUDOR CLOTHES

MEN

Clothes depended on the work a man did and how wealthy he was. All men wore shirts. Those of the nobility and wealthy were made of silk, the shirts of others were made of wool or linen. Over the shirt, men wore a garment called a doublet. This was sometimes sleeveless and sometimes had tight fitting, detachable sleeves. Nobles and the wealthy wore doublets made of expensive materials with elaborate patterns. Others wore doublets made of wool or a rough canvas material called kersey.

Until 1540 all men wore tights known as hose which stretched from the waist to the feet. Unlike modern tights, hose were not held up by elastic (not invented until 19th century). Laces were passed through holes in both garments and tied. Hose showed the outline of the thighs and legs but the genitals were protected by a bag called a codpiece attached to the hose by laces.

Over the doublet, nobles, wealthy and middle-class men wore a robe or gown reaching from the shoulder to well below the knee. Husbandmen and labourers wore a woollen jerkin or jacket which was a coat with sleeves reaching from the shoulder to the knee. This jerkin was fastened at the waist by a belt. Some men of high fashion also wore a jerkin made with expensive materials.

Shoes worn by the wealthy changed with fashion becoming wider and less pointed in the early 16th century. Sometimes they were fastened by a strap across the instep, sometimes they were tight fitting. Gentlemen wore boots for riding and walking outdoors. Labourers also wore boots for working in the fields.

Men of all classes wore caps, bonnets and hats at all times. Husbandmen and artisans wore small, round, woollen bonnets, fashionable noblemen and gentlemen wore felt hats often with feathers. All wore hats and caps indoors even at meals. In the evenings at home with their families men changed into their nightgowns (very much like a dressing gown today) and put on nightcaps. They wore nightcaps all evening but changed them for simple linen caps when they went to bed.

After 1540 the hose which had been fashionable for 350 years was replaced by breeches. There was a brief, intermediary time between about 1540 - 1570 when men wore trunk hose. These were tight below the knee but from the thigh to the knee they were loose and baggy, and were often padded. By 1575 trunk hose had been discarded for Venetian breeches simply called 'Venetians'. These breeches, more elaborate than the upper part of trunk hose, reached to the knee, leaving the bottom part of the trunk hose as stockings. Breeches remained fashionable for nearly 300 years until they were replaced by trousers in the 19th century.

After 1540 other fashions changed. Noblemen and gentlemen abandoned the gown and wore a shorter sleeveless cloak instead. The flat cap of Henry VIII's reign was replaced after 1560 by a high bonnet sometimes as high as six inches above the head with a feather on the side of it. After 1540 the narrow band at the neck previously only an inch wide and just visitble grew into a pleated collar. This became more elaborate until by 1570 it had been replaced by a ruff. This was a detachable collar, some three inches wide, fitting over the shirt and all around the neck. This ruff grew even larger until by the end of the Tudor period it covered the whole width of the shoulders.

Before 1550 Tudor men were normally clean-shaven but after this time beards were fashionable and worn by most gentlemen and noblemen.

WOMEN

Upper class women wore dresses down to the ground with tight fitting or loose sleeves reaching to the wrist. At the beginning of the Tudor period, they wore a bodice and skirt called a kertie under the dress. The neckline was low and square cut. Women wore a tight fitting undercap and over it a hood called the gable hood. This completely covered the hair, went down to the shoulders and half way down the back. After 1525 the French hood became fashionable the only difference being the front of the head was uncovered showing the ladies' hair. As the Tudor age proceeded the low necklines were replaced by high collars which hid the neck from view. After 1560 women began wearing the same ruffs as men.

After 1540 the kertle was divided into two parts. A support jutting out from the waist became fashionable. This was called a Spanish farthingale and the skirt or petticoat went over this. After 1580 the Spanish farthingale was replaced by the French farthingale. The French version had hoops under the skirt which made it stand out for two feet on both sides of the waist and then fall vertically to the ankles. Dresses were not quite so long as previously. The French farthingale stayed fashionable until the end of the Tudor period. Slim waists were in vogue and ladies wore corsets stiffened with wood or iron. Stomachs were kept flat by using stomachers, which had a V-shaped panel of stiff material.

Women wore hats throughout the period when travelling outdoors. These were worn over the undercap and were often high-crowned with feathers and jewelled headbands.

Working class women tended to wear shorter dresses than the wealthy. They often rolled up their sleeves when working.

Unmarried women sometimes wore their hair loose and flowing over their shoulders, fastened only by a ribbon. Married working class women covered their hair with a simple linen headdress.

TUDOR CLOTHES

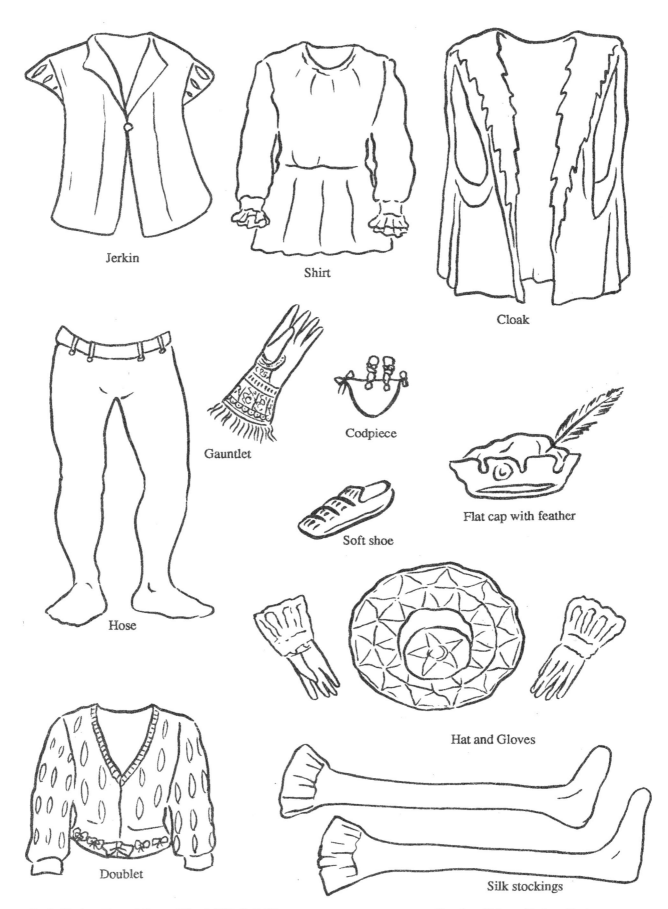

Jerkin

Shirt

Cloak

Hose

Gauntlet

Codpiece

Flat cap with feather

Soft shoe

Hat and Gloves

Doublet

Silk stockings

CHILDREN

In general children were dressed in the same way as their parents. They looked lke young adults.

Girls, like their brothers, were always dressed like miniature adults. In early Tudor times, this meant that they wore long, loose-fitting gowns, with very wide fur-trimmed sleeves. To be fashionable, the neck-line was square, and cut low enough for a brightly coloured undergarment or a frilled chemise to show as an edging.

By the reign of Elizabeth it had become fashionable for girls to wear farthingales. A farthingale was a series of hoops made of cane, whalebone or wire, sewn into a petticoat to make the dress stand out. (Poorer girls made their dresses stand out in the same way, but more cheaply by tying a long roll of padding around their hips. This roll was known as a bum roll.) Huge ruffs and large padded shoulders also became popular with the wealthy as did jewelled bodices coming to a deep V at the waist in the front. They also liked to have an inverted V opening in the front of their shirts, from waist to hem, which would reveal a special underskirt made of some elaborate, contrasting material.

By the age of 15 many girls belonging to wealthy parents were married, (A girl was legally allowed to marry at 12 and a boy at 14.) Romantic love usually had nothing to do with such a marriage. It was merely arranged by the couple's parents in order to enlarge or improve their estates or wealth.

Discuss fashion with the children and the changes in fashion. Youngsters become fashion conscious at a very early age. Recent changes include jeans and the partial demise of the raincoat, hats and gloves. Discuss Tudor fashion and what people wore. Include hair styles and for men include beards. Discuss the speed at which fashion changed then and now.

Let the children cut out drawings of clothes and paste them on drawings of men and women. Make dolls using pipe cleaners, pieces of wire or rolls of newspaper and dress them with pieces of material to make Tudor dolls. Let children draw pictures of hats, gloves, shoes and jewellery worn by the Tudors. Remember that in Tudor times men and women wore jewellery around their necks and on their hands. Discuss this fashion with the children. Let them design a piece of jewellery. Show the children portraits of Tudor men and women from all classes so that they can see what they wore. Let them see how fashions changed and were changing from 1500 to 1600.

Use the drawing below to illustrate how Queen Elizabeth I dressed. She loved to be 'fashionable' and she highlights the changes in women's clothes that occurred in her reign. Discuss her special delight in silk stockings. The illustration also shows the fashion of wearing the hair up: this was often frizzed, pulled back from the hairline and decorated with jewellery. Note too, the pointed, low waisted bodice. This was another feature of the dress of wealthy women towards the end of the Tudor period. The children might like to make a Queen Elizabeth doll.

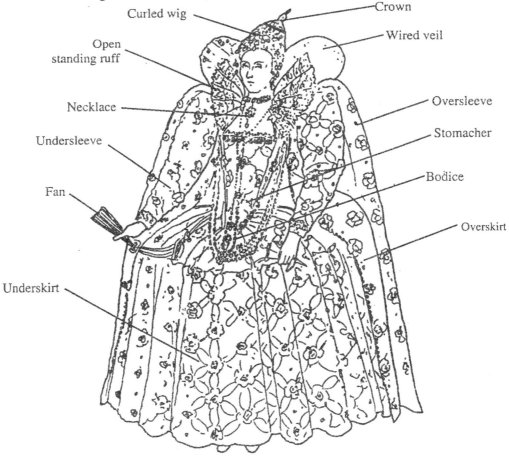

Queen Elizabeth

SPORTS AND PASTIMES

SPORTS AND PASTIMES

Since the Middle Ages noblemen engaged in **tournaments**. Knights jousted against each other watched by admiring audiences. **Jousting** was still popular in Tudor times but by now the combatants were protected by heavy suits of armour and lances were more easily broken to avoid injuring the participants. Henry VII was not interested in this sport but his son, Henry VIII, enjoyed the sport for the first twenty-six years of his reign. Royal jousting ended on 24 January, 1536, however, when the King was thrown from his horse and lay unconscious for two hours. (The dangers may be illustrated by the fate of the French King, Henry II who died in a Paris tournament in 1559 when a piece of the lance he was carrying splintered and penetrated his eye through a slit in his visor.)

Another popular sport in Tudor times was called **riding at the ring**. This entailed a rider on horseback-carrying a lance riding at full gallop at a ring only a few inches wide suspended on a thread. The aim was to put the point of the lance through the ring and carry it away. **Hunting** was another royal sport, usually for a stag (the Tudors called it a hart). Hunting took place throughout the year except during the harsh winter months when **hawking** was the main traditional sport. Falcons were trained to hunt and bring their quarry back to their trainer. Finally, as far as the upper classes were concerned there was **archery** and Henry VIII was a very good archer. But from the beginning of Tudor times there was great concern about the decline of this sport and Parliament tried to encourage it.

Indoors, the upper classes played many games. **Chess**, in particular, was popular and new rules were brought in which have lasted until today. **Gambling at cards** and **dice** were also popular, the most usual game being **cent** (modern piquet). Another pastime was **dancing**. Henry VIII loved to dance and so did his daughter, Elizabeth. When she was queen, Elizabeth enjoyed dancing the pavane, a stately, elegant step. The galliard was also a favourite but the volta in which the gentleman clasped the lady around the waist and lifted her into the air was the most popular and daring of them all. Other pastimes which needed music and which were popular with monarchs and nobility throughout Tudor times and the 17th century were **masques** and **pageants**. Masques were dramatic entertainments in which the participants wore masks and costumes and took part in pantomime, dancing, dialogue and songs. They were held indoors. The themes were usually stories from Greek mythology, the bible or allegorical praising chastity and virtue. Pageants were similar to masques but took place outdoors. They were colourful parades portraying scenes from history and were often used by Tudor monarchs as a means of spreading propaganda (e.g. in Elizabeth's coronation procession a pageant extolled the virtues of Protestantism and the bible in English).

Stage plays became important in the Tudor period. First acted by strolling players in inn yards, they often had religious themes. These were the 'miracle' and 'morality' plays that were inherited from the Middle Ages. These were followed in Henry VIII's day by light comedy *(Ralph Roister Doister)* and coarse farce *(Gammer Gurton's Nedle)*. In Elizabeth's time there were the magnificent plays of Marlowe and Shakespeare. It was then that playhouses began to be built and actors depended less on travelling from one venue to another. It was the age of the new theatres: the *Curtain*, the *Rose*, the *Swan* and the *Globe*.

There were numerous other games and pastimes in the 16th century which must be mentioned. Many of these were outlawed or forbidden as far as the lower classes were concerned but most people still indulged. Many of them were cruel sports and pastimes but it must be remembered that in many ways the Tudor age was a cruel one.

One of the most popular was **bear-baiting** loved by commoner and nobleman alike. The bear was tied by its legs to a post using a long chain and fierce dogs were set on it. The dogs tried to tear out the bear's throat whilst the bear defended itself. The bear and dogs fought until the dogs were killed or the bear fatally injured. Another spectator sport was **cock-fighting**. Two trained fighting cocks fought each other until one was killed or too injured to fight any longer. London had many cockpits and huge sums were wagered on which cocks would win.

Other games which were played included **tennis** and **bowls**. The Tudor version of tennis was very different from today's game. It was played indoors with hand-strung rackets and balls made of leather shells stuffed with hair. (See illustrations in Children's Worksheets.) Another popular, but illegal game, was **'fotebal'**. The ball was a pig's bladder. Again, this differed from today's game. The object of the game was to put the ball through the opponents' goal: the goals might be two or three miles apart. Two teams from nearby villages agreed to meet somewhere between them. There were no other rules. The ball could be kicked or thrown. Players could pick up the ball and run with it and they could be stopped by holding, punching, tripping or tackling. There was no limit to the number of players and all the young men in a village and even the women could join in. Players were often seriously hurt. **Wrestling** was another rough and popular Tudor game.

Other games and amusements (some are still played today) were **hop-scotch**, **hide and seek**, **leap-frog** and **blind man's buff**. **Billiards** was played in large houses. The game of **shuttlecocks** was played and people

flew kites. In a game called **nine-holes**, balls were rolled into holes in the ground or on a specially made board. **Handy-dandy** was a guessing game. One person hid a small stone in his or her hand and the other player had to guess which hand had the stone. Men played a game similar to golf called **bandy-bar**. Others **pitched the bar** which was very much like tossing the caber. Indoor games included **draughts, shuffleboard** (shove ha'penny) **and backgammon** (known as **tables**).

Country folk liked country fairs with sideshows and jugglers, acrobats, fire-eaters and dancing bears … They enjoyed gay jigs, hornpipes and morris dancing. On May Day, a young tree was cut down and decorated with flowers and herbs and coloured string to make a Maypole. People danced around it and feasted. From 1595 smoking emerged as a popular habit. Drake had brought tobacco back in 1585 and this new commodity soon caught on.

MUSIC

Music was a very popular pastime in the 16th century and every educated person was expected to be able to read it. At the beginning of the period the only sort available was church music and this was used for dancing and in songs. There were, of course, folk songs and after 1550 new hymns were composed. By 1579 William Byrd was writing music about spring and love. People entertained themselves and their families by singing songs and playing musical instruments. (See Children's Worksheets for drawings of some Tudor musical instruments.)

Discuss Tudor sports and pastimes with the children. Explain that many of these were remnants from the Middle Ages. Show how the Tudors were emerging from these earlier times. Explain words like tournaments and jousts and describe a typical tournament. In many ways Henry VIII was a medieval knight - he participated.

Examine the problems of dangerous sports, then and now. Remember that the Tudor period was the time of the horse and show how many sports and pastimes involved horses e.g. tournaments, riding at the ring and hunting. Learning to ride was an activity in itself. Remember the importance of archery and discuss why Parliament wanted to see archery maintained. If possible let the children see a longbow, crossbow and arquebus. Explain the differences. Show the children a chess set. Some may already play or like to learn. Explain the names of the pieces. Compare and contrast Tudor dancing with traditional dancing and with dancing today. Play Tudor music to the children. Do they like it? Explain what is meant by a masque and pageant. Let the children make their own masks and if possible engage them in a masque for role play.

Let the children research Elizabethan theatre, especially the *Globe*. If possible let them visit the reconstructed *Globe* to learn about Tudor theatre at first hand. Pinpoint Christopher Marlow and William Shakespeare. Tell the children about Shakespeare's life and work. Let them see a Shakespearean play. Compare a visit to the theatre in Tudor times and now. Let the children look at the script of a miracle or morality play emphasizing good and bad, with good triumphing over evil.

Discuss cruel games including bear-baiting and cock-fighting. Examine arguments for and against. Compare sports and pastimes in Tudor times with those today, especially Tudor' fotebal' and modern football, tennis then and now. Examine the rules of the games.

Let the children play some of the games such as Handy-Dandy and Blind Man's Buff. If possible let the children learn morris dancing. Let the children create a Maypole on paper or on a collage. Discuss Tudor music and the musical instruments they used. Compare and contrast with today.

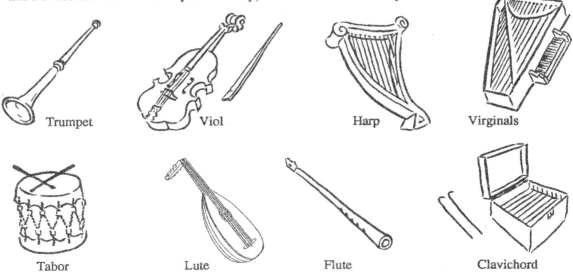

Trumpet   Viol   Harp   Virginals

Tabor   Lute   Flute   Clavichord

16th Century Musical Instruments

MEDICINE AND HEALTH
IN TUDOR TIMES

MEDICINE

It is remarkable that the Greek Physician, Galen, (130 - 200 AD) was the leading authority on medicine throughout the Tudor period. Sir Thomas Elyot who wrote a book on medicine in 1541 called *The Castle of Health* and John Kaye, Elizabeth I's court physician both followed Galen. Doctors were keen on dieting and blood-letting. The belief following Galen was that diseases could be cured by getting rid of bad blood. Bleeding was accomplished by venupuncture from a vein or by placing leeches on the patient's body.

There was a distinction between physicians and barber-surgeons. The physicians were mainly theoretical doctors extolling virtuous living and good diet. They were learned people who wrote books rather than dealt with patients. The duties they performed were ecclesiastic and diplomatic rather than medical or clinical. The practical exponents of medicine were the barber-surgeons. They performed surgical operations, pulled teeth, set bones, straightened fractures and amputated arms and legs. Surgery was performed without anaesthetics, the patient being plied with alcohol and held down by the barber-surgeon's helpers. Wounds were cauterized by applying burning oil or boiling oil to the wound. (Ambroise Paré, the French surgeon,1510 - 1590, first treated wounds with an ointment of egg yolk, rose oil and turpentine which eventually improved matters but this did not reach English medicine for 50 years.) Apothecaries were men skilled in herbal cures.

Doctors in Tudor times still believed in the ancient theory of disease in which there were four humours and four qualities. The humours were blood, phlegm, white bile and black bile. These coincided with the temperaments sanguine, phlegmatic, choleric and melancholic. The four qualities were cold, hot, moist and dry. All matter was thought to consist of earth, air, fire and water. These theories are represented diagrammatically below

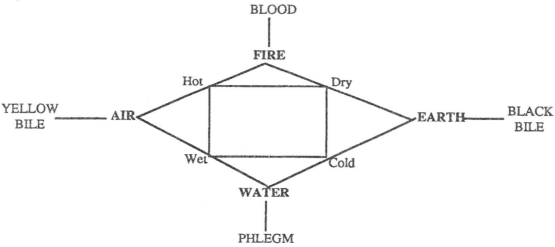

Clinical diagnosis and judgements were made on these theories. Thus, doctors described the beneficial effects of eating eggs and other foods and the harm that could be done by over-stimulation, eating leeks, onions, garlic and taking too much pepper. Old people were phlegmatic (cold and moist) and should avoid eating lamb. All fruit was bad and caused bad humours while milk was good for students as they tended to be melancholic.

DISEASES

Smallpox and measles were new diseases in Tudor times and the medical profession had no means of treating them. All doctors could do was to wait for the diseases 'to go'. Other new diseases included syphilis and the 'sweating sickness'. The last-named reached London in September, 1485 after Henry VII's victory at Bosworth. It was characterised by profuse sweating and the patients died within ten or twelve hours. Women seldom caught it. The sweating sickness returned from time to time and was particularly virulent in 1517, 1528 and 1551. It was very much like the epidemics of influenza which have ravaged Europe since 1919 to the present day.

Although the sweating sickness was bad, plague and cholera were even more serious and killed many more victims. There were several outbreaks of plague in the reign of Henry VIII. The most serious occurred in Elizabeth's reign when 17,046 people died in London alone between June 1563 and June 1564. The plague

returned several times in her reign but the worse epidemic was in the year the Queen died (1603) when 38,000 Londoners died. Characterised by lumps in the neck and under the armpits, there was no cure. The only action was to keep those infected away from others. Houses where cases had occurred were marked with a blue cross on white paper and the words, *Lord, have mercy upon us.* All the doors and windows were to remain closed for forty days.

[It was, of course, not known at the time that the plague was spread by fleas living on rats or that cholera was spread by water contaminated by human waste. The living conditions of the Tudors provided an ideal environment for these diseases.]

HEALTH AND HYGIENE

The Tudors knew little about medicine and even less about hygiene. Their houses had no plumbing and water was always in short supply. Houses were built as close as possible to a supply of fresh water - near a lake, river, stream or brook - which meant that it was soon polluted with sewage and refuse. People began to rely on natural springs and rivers away from the centres of population. Others relied on water brought by water-carriers but even then they could not be sure that the water was clean.

Housewives usually threw their rubbish into the street or into the local river. Outside lavatories were built over water or situated some distance from the houses. Inside, people used chamber pots and stool rooms. These were buckets under stools with holes in the seats. The pots and buckets were emptied into holes in the earth called cesspits but they were infested with flies and created unpleasant smells. People were responsible for clearing the space in front of their houses. However, dunghills piled up in the streets and workers called scavengers were employed to remove them in their muck carts. But it was a constant battle and pigs, dogs and rats dug into the piles of muck which were ideal breeding areas for disease.

People seldom bathed and even 'Good Queen Bess' only had one or two baths a year. When they did bath, water was so scarce they shared. Soap was available, a homemade mixture of fats and ashes, which was hard and unpleasant. Bathing water was scented with herbs to make people smell sweeter. Clothes were unkempt and dirty and were not often washed. People rarely cleaned their teeth but when they did they used a soft cloth, not a brush. There was no toothpaste and as people liked to eat sweet things, many had bad or broken teeth. Queen Elizabeth's teeth were black before she reached middle age.

By the end of the 16th century, ideas had begun to change. Preparatory work in scientific method and improvements in equipment and techniques laid the basis for the remarkable discoveries of the 17th century associated with Harvey, Francis Bacon, Descartes, Boyle and above all, Isaac Newton.

Discuss medicine, diagnosis, disease and health and hygiene in Tudor times with the children. Explain how the medical profession and others believed in the mumbo-jumbo and arrant nonsense invented by the Greeks and that this was relied on for 2,000 years. Compare and contrast the way the sick were treated then and now. Discuss the roles of physicians, barber-surgeons and apothecaries. Outline the main diseases especially cholera, plague and sweating sickness. Discuss how the plague was spread. Compare and contrast public health problems then and now, how town councils deal with possible health hazards today. Discuss the provision of water, electricity and gas today and compare with the facilities the Tudors had. Explain how the Tudors washed and how they heated their homes.

Flea and
Rat
(Not to scale)

The Plague (Black Death)

THE TUDOR POOR

BEGGARS AND VAGABONDS, POOR LAW

A lasting problem throughout the 16th century was the problem of poverty. Some have estimated that over half the population were destitute. Certainly, there were huge numbers of beggars, rogues, thieves, vagabonds and hangers on.

REASONS FOR UNEMPLOYMENT

1. A legacy from the Wars of the Roses. Many soldiers discharged from military service had no work.
2. The problem in 1 was made worse by Henry VII's firm enforcement of the statute against livery and maintenance. This meant nobles were no longer allowed to keep armed retainers in their service and these men swelled the ranks of the unemployed.
3. Some were sailors who did not have a ship. One voyage over, they could not get another.
4. Enclosures, the conversion of arable land into pasture land (sheep and wool were now more profitable), caused widespread unemployment amongst farmers and husbandmen (farm labourers).
5. Those who had worked on the land for a pittance refused to go back to it.
6. Many refused to work as artisans in the towns.
7. The dissolution of the monasteries was a major cause. The confiscation of monastic lands, together with the properties of the guilds, chantries and hospitals brought about extensive changes in the demand for labour. Not only were monks, nuns and priests out of work but there were thousands of people whom they had employed who now had no places to go.
8. The restrictions imposed by the guilds on industry and employment.
9. Old industries declined and new ones which sprang up demanded only skilled labour.
10. A rise in the population which began in Henry VIII's day.
11. The debasement of the coinage - the fall in the value of money - which lasted from 1527 - 1550 (and the effects which lasted until the end of the Tudor period) did not help matters.
12. The influx of silver from Spanish mines in the New World meant a rise in the cost of living and in the prices of basic commodities such as food.

The problem was not confined to the labouring classes. The statutes of the time referred to others like university students who became rogues and vagabonds. The Tudors divided the poor into two categories.

THE IMPOTENT POOR These were people who were unable to work because they were too old, had been injured in war, shipwrecked, suffered from a disease and so on. They were the blind, the one-legged or one armed ... They were deemed to be fit objects for Christian charity.

THE ABLE-BODIED POOR These were regarded as idlers, the rogues and vagabonds of Tudor society. The opinion was that such people did not want to work or were avoiding work, and because of this they were not to be pitied but deserved to be punished.

LEGISLATION in the early Tudor period consisted of two Vagrancy Acts passed in 1496 and 1504. The aim of these was to make sure the impotent poor returned to the place of their birth where they could get help and relief and to punish able-bodied beggars by confining them to the stocks. Legislation throughout the period followed the same pattern: help for the impotent poor and punishment (more rigorously as time went on) for those considered to be idlers and wasters.

Able-bodied beggars, vagrants and vagabonds came in for harsh treatment as Tudor government tried strenuously to deal with the problem. They could be whipped, imprisoned, branded with a hot iron, have a ear cut off or be put into slavery or sentenced to death.

Under Elizabeth, the first system of Poor-Law Relief evolved. In 1563 the First Poor-Law made contributions for the relief of the poor compulsory. In 1572 the Second Poor-Law appointed officials to collect the contributions. It was no longer left to the individual to assess himself. *Habitations for the impotent and aged were to be built.* Vagabonds were to be *grieviously whipped.* In 1597 and 1601 the Third and Fourth Poor-Laws set up the system which lasted until 1834. Each parish nominated overseers who had the power to tax all the inhabitants of that parish for the relief of the poor.

By the end of the period the aged and impotent poor were to be sent to houses for the poor called 'Abiding Places'. The idea of the Workhouse which only changed in the 20th century had been born. It is true to say that the Tudors never solved the problem of the poor or poor relief.

Discuss the attitude to poverty in Tudor times with the children. Let them express their views on how the poor should be treated. Outline how the Tudors tried to deal with the problems and how society looks after the poor and aged today. Mention the welfare state and the 'free' National Health Service. Consider the reasons for people becoming the 'impotent' poor and the reasons why people did not (and do not) want to work.

CRIME AND PUNISHMENT
CRIME

In Tudor times there was a great deal of crime. The crimes were often personal because there were thousands of people out of work who were homeless and starving. Petty theft, daylight robberies and burglary were commonplace and there were many murders. Then there were crimes which had religious or political motives. These were riot, treason and rebellion: there were at least eight major rebellions against government in the Tudor period.

LOCAL FORCES AGAINST CRIME There was, of course, no paid national police force. Crime prevention and control were in the hands of the sheriffs, Justices of the Peace, local constables and ordinary law-abiding citizens. The sheriff was responsible for arresting criminals and holding them in custody in the local jail. JPs tried people accused of crimes in the local courts. It was JPs too who proclaimed the 'hue and cry' when every inhabitant of a parish was expected to turn out to hunt criminals. If a convicted criminal escaped, the parish was liable to a fine.

LAWLESS AREAS Particular areas of the country were more lawless than others, e.g. the roads from London to Henley-on-Thames and from London to Reading passed through an area called 'The Thicket', an ideal place for highway robbery. Thieves attacked travellers as they passed by. There were areas in the country where laws were almost impossible to enforce. These included Wales and parts of Northumberland.

POLITICAL CRIME was important during Tudor times but much of this had religious or economic connotations. For example, there were serious riots in London when aliens were attacked in 1517. These were called the 'Evil May Day' riots. Then there were the rebellions.

REBELLIONS
1. **Pilgrimage of Grace (1536 - 7).** This was a northern rising due to political discontent among the gentry, agrarian unrest caused by enclosures and high rents. The rebellion spread to Yorkshire and Lincolnshire. Robert Aske was the leader in Yorkshire protesting against monastic closures.
2. **Kett's Rebellion (1549).** This was a rebellion which tried to gain government support against agrarian changes including enclosures and encroachments on common lands.
3. **Wyatt's Rebellion (1554).** This was an attempt to uphold Protestantism and to prevent the proposed unpopular marriage between Queen Mary Tudor and Philip II of Spain.
4. **Robert Devereux** led a revolt in London in 1601 to protect himself against members of the Privy Council planning to arrest and assassinate him.

TREASON There were numerous acts of treason against the monarch by individuals and groups. Examples of these are Perkin Warbeck and Lambert Simnel in Henry VII's reign, the attempt to put Lady Jane Grey on the throne at the beginning of Mary's reign in 1553 and the numerous attempts, with the connivance of pro-Catholics and Spaniards to kill Elizabeth and put Mary Queen of Scots on the throne (see Northern Earls, Ridolfi and Babington plots).

As far as major rebellions were concerned the Tudors were at a disadvantage because they did not have a standing army. They could not call on a large force of military men to help them. The only soldiers they had were the 'Yeomen of the Guard'. These were created by Henry VII in 1485 as a corps of 50 men and the number was increased by Henry VIII to 600 in 1520. In times of trouble and rebellion the Tudors relied on a system which had existed from feudal times. Basically, this was a call to arms: the nobles were ordered to summon the gentlemen in their area to come with their tenants to the aid of the monarch. The numbers of horsemen, infantrymen and bowmen called and where they were to meet was decided by the monarch.

PUNISHMENT

Many of the punishments were a legacy from medieval times. Crimes of treason, rebellion, riot and murder and stealing were all punished by death. Death came in a number of ways - by the gallows, by execution with an axe or with a sword. Nobility had a choice, and Anne Boleyn chose the sword.

TORTURE It was hard to prove guilt so various methods of torture were used to exact confessions. Thumb screws and the rack were used as well as hot pokers which were thrust up the anus (death often resulted through shock). The rack stretched the prisoner's joints. There was also a device called the 'Scavenger's Daughter' which squeezed the prisoner tighter and tighter.

PUNISHMENTS for minor crimes included being put in the stocks, being whipped, being branded, being pilloried or put in a ducking stool. Offending thieves might have their hands cut off and more serious offenders

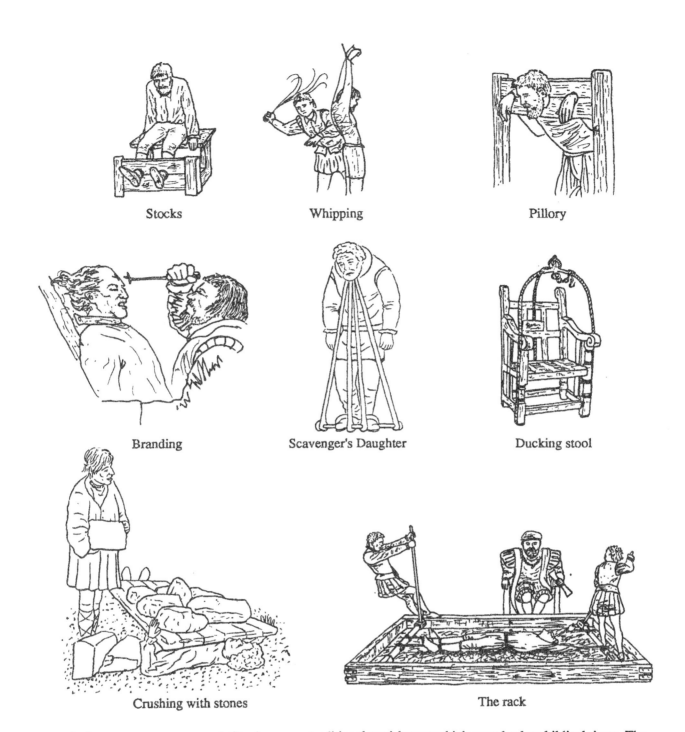

Stocks

Whipping

Pillory

Branding

Scavenger's Daughter

Ducking stool

Crushing with stones

The rack

had eyes or tongue removed. Stoning was a traditional punishment which went back to biblical times. The Tudors invented a new method in which the prisoner was made to lie down and stones were heaped on him until he was crushed to death. Those imprisoned in the Tower or elsewhere might find themselves in an oubliette. This was a prison within a prison, a small confined space where prisoners were left and forgotten. They usually died from starvation.

Discuss crime and punishment with the children and outline the types and methods of punishment. Make sure they know what is meant by the stocks and the pillory. Discuss unjust punishments for minor crimes. Examine the reasons for the extent of lawlessness in Tudor times and now. Let the children suggest reasons for crime. Compare Tudor crimes with today's. Remember the role of the Tower of London and death by the sword or axe for nobles. Remember too, the mighty power of the monarch who could imprison, torture and execute at will. Discuss the pros and cons of the death penalty. Make a chart showing the variety of punishments that existed.

You will have to decide whether to discuss this with very young children. Remember that some may get nightmares and others may want to experiment with some of the methods!

THE TUDOR NAVY
THE SHIPS

HENRY VII had little interest in developing the navy. He had just five royal ships. These included two new four-masted carracks, large trading, sailing ships with two or four masts. This small fleet was administered by one official, the 'Clerk of the King's Ships'. The traditional enemy at this time, France, was already building up her maritime strength. In Henry VII's time warships were mainly troop carriers. Battles at sea were fought by closing with enemy ships and boarding them. The soldiers (marines) then fought on the ships as if they were on land: ships were floating troop carriers.

HENRY VIII was very interested in ships and the navy. Intent on winning military glory almost as soon as he took over the reins of government he ordered one of his father's carracks to be rebuilt and two more constructed according to the latest European designs. Henry wanted a navy strong enough to hold the Channel and blockade the enemy while he invaded France. The King was personally fascinated by ships. He had some technical knowledge and always asked for reports on the progress and performance of new vessels. He learned about several novel ship designs and ordered the building of warships armed with batteries of cannon which could fire through ports cut in the ships' sides. These were designed to break the resistance of enemy vessels by bombarding them with cannon shot. Henry's naval ambitions made him encourage gunfounders. Ship builders set up new gun foundries and brought experts from abroad. Soon, English guns and ammunition rivalled those of Germany, France and Italy.

The King enjoyed himself on his new ships. He loved to play the part of a ship's master, dressing up in naval costume - cloth of gold and scarlet hose - and blowing shrill blasts on a bosun's pipe or whistle hung around his neck on a gold chain. Henry also liked ship-board banquets.

In 1509, the only naval dockyard was at Portsmouth. As the navy grew, Henry established new bases at Deptford, Woolwich and Erith on the Thames. At first, he appointed people to look after these new bases and ships on a day-to-day basis but later (1545 - 6) he set up the 'King's Majesty Council of the Marine'. This was the origin of the Admiralty. The council was responsible for the administration of the fleet, finances and the supply of weapons.

The invention of hinged, watertight gunports, at the beginning of the century meant that guns could be carried low in the ships. This helped stability and there was less risk of straining the timbers. The *Mary Rose*, 600 tons, was the first English ship to carry these new guns and fight at sea by the new methods (firing broadsides to damage and if possible sink enemy ships rather than closing and boarding). In 1510 the *Mary Rose* was probably equipped with gunports on the main deck and there were two major refits in 1527 and in 1536. As early as March 1513 when the King reviewed the fleet at Greenwich, the *Mary Rose* was pronounced the best and fastest in the fleet.

The most expensive naval project was the building of the *Henry Grace à Dieu* or *Great Harry*. Launched in 1514 she was the biggest ship in the world. She was armed with 21 heavy guns of bronze and 231 lighter pieces and had a crew of 700 men. The largest warship afloat, she probably weighed some 1,200 tons. She had four masts and sails made of gold cloth for state occasions. Unfortunately, she was destroyed by accident in a fire on the Thames in 1553.

Earlier, a naval battle had resulted in the loss of another of Henry's pride and joy. On 18 July, 1545 (28 July by the modern calendar), Henry had a huge pre-battle banquet on the *Great Harry*. 60 English ships were prepared for a French attack. This was the Battle of the Solent. The first day's fighting was indecisive, the second day went to the French but suddenly the wind changed and the French were routed. The great disaster of the day was the loss of the *Mary Rose*. The ship was lost through folly and insubordination. Weighed down by heavy guns as she turned about she heeled to one side and sea water poured through gunports left open after firing. From the shore the King watched in dismay as hundreds of terrified men sank to their deaths.

In times of crisis, Henry VIII increased his ship building programme. Peak periods of building were 1512 - 14, 1522 - 5, 1539 and 1544 - 6. By the time he died in 1547 the King had built up the fleet to over 50 ships, had established new dockyards and had founded a new administration to take care of his fleet.

Little attention was paid to the navy in the short reigns of Edward VI and Mary Tudor and the next developments occurred in the reign of Elizabeth I.

ELIZABETH I owed much of her naval strength and strategies to the efforts of her sailors. These included Sir John Hawkins, Sir Martin Frobisher, Sir Richard Grenville and Sir Francis Drake. These men had become skilled in naval warfare against the Spanish in the Netherlands and in the New World. By the time of the Armada (1588) the total English force consisted of 197 ships. Most of these were smaller than the Spanish ships, though no ship of the Armada was as large as Frobisher's vessel, the *Triumph* (1,100 tons). Some of the English ships were very small indeed, only 35 tons. Sir John Hawkins had, however, overhauled and modernized the fleet by 1588. The English ships were more manoeuverable and English cannon had a

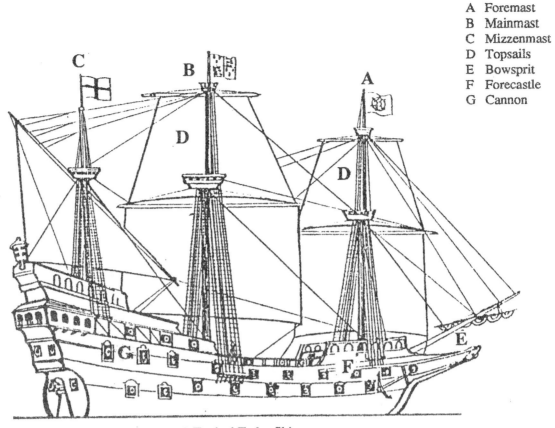

A Typical Tudor Ship

longer range. This prevented the Spaniards from pursuing their tactics of coming alongside, throwing grappling hooks to hold a ship and then board for marines to fight hand-to-hand on deck. Events proved that the guns of the English ships' were superior in close-range bombardment.

By the end of the Tudor period the navy had proved itself to be an effective fighting force.

LIFE AT SEA

LIVING QUARTERS Life at sea in Tudor times was very hard. Sailors faced death from battle, accidents and disease. Their floating home was damp, dark and overcrowded. The way in which seamen lived on board depended on their rank. The captain and his officers fared much better than ordinary seamen. The officers had richly furnished cabins and their own supplies of food including expensive imported commodites and spices. Ordinary seamen lived in cramped conditions and sometimes there was hardly room for them to lie down. Their quarters were in the forecastle of the ships which was often dark and smelly.

FOOD Sailors lived on dried and salted meat and/or fish, biscuit (a hard, slow baked mixture of flour and water), butter and cheese. They drank beer because this kept better than water. With no refrigeration, on long voyages meat soon became rotten and full of maggots while the biscuit became riddled with weevils. Sailors described black headed maggots *as fat and cold to the taste* while *weevils were bitter*. A young boy said he was glad they ate when it was dark so that he could not see them in his food. Also on long voyages, the seamen had no fresh vegetables or fruit. This meant they did not eat enough vitamin C and suffered from scurvy with anaemia and bleeding beneath the skin.

GOING INTO BATTLE on a wooden Tudor vessel must have been exciting but terrifying. Especially frightening must have been the attempts of the enemy to get close before they released their fire or to be the first to receive a deadly blast. The cries of wounded comrades, the smell of blood and burning gunpowder were all around. The crews loading, aiming and firing the guns were at risk. They could be killed instantly, have limbs severed or be badly cut by flying splinters.

DISCIPLINE was strict and punishment was harsh. Flogging was usual and sailors were whipped for minor offences. They could also be clapped in irons or keelhauled. The last punishment involved dragging a sailor by a rope from one side of a vessel to the other through the water under the keel.

THE 'MARY ROSE'

This is a unique and important primary source, a time capsule of Tudor life. Built at Portsmouth in 1510 the *Mary Rose* was Henry VIII's battleship which carried over 400 soldiers and sailors. It sank in a battle fought off Portsmouth against the French in 1545.

In 1982 the *Mary Rose*, partly preserved in silt, was lifted from the bed of the Solent, together with the weapons, cargo and the personal possessions of the unfortunate crew. The ship is now on show in Portsmouth dockyard. Visitors can get an impression of its comparative compactness (32 metres in length) and the craftsmanship involved in its construction. It was built from an estimated 36 acres of felled forest.

The exhibition shows the cannons, swords and bows and arrows the crew were carrying into battle and also the everyday items of life from the Tudor period. These include caps and boots, games such as backgammon sets, musical instruments, surgeon's tools and numerous pots and pans as well as the bones of a small dog and a baby rat. Although quills were found on board, most of the crew would have been illiterate, and to help them with tasks such as fitting the correct cover to the correct hatch, pictogram-like marks were used.

DATA

1509 - 1511   The *Mary Rose* was built in Portsmouth on the orders of King Henry VIII.

1536   Rebuilt with new and more efficient guns.

19 July, 1545   Sank at the Battle of the Solent.

1836   Divers John and Charles Deane discovered the site of the submerged 'Mary Rose' and recovered a bronze demi-cannon gun.

1965 - 1971   Amateur divers searched for the *Mary Rose* on the sea bed using sonar equipment. A programme of exploration and survey was undertaken.

1979   The *Mary Rose* Trust was formed to totally excavate, record and prepare the ship for recovery.

1982   On 11 October, 1982, the *Mary Rose* was brought to the surface.

1982 - today   Work continues to preserve the *Mary Rose* and the objects found on her. She has become a unique, rich, historical source for scholars and the general public.

HISTORICAL IMPORTANCE OF THE 'MARY ROSE'

Much can be learned from this priceless, primary source. These are a few suggestions but the list is almost endless.

1. Details of how ships were built in the 16th century such as the wood used and how they were manned and sailed.
2. Details of how ships were designed in the 16th century - forecastles, aftercastles, number of masts and so on.
3. Information about the different types of vessels: carracks, caravels, galleons and so on.
4. Details of how ships like the *Mary Rose* were designed for naval warfare and the armaments they carried.
5. How sailors lived and where they were accommodated aboard the vessel.
6. Differences between the lifestyles of officers and ordinary seamen.
7. The diet of the men on board.
8. Details of the clothes worn by the crew.
9. Details about discipline and punishment on board.
10. Details about the pastimes of the officers and ordinary seamen.
11. Information about important people on board such as the master, the barber surgeon, the cook ...
12. Details about religion and worship on board.
13. Details about illness and disease on board and how sickness and injuries were treated.
14. Information about accounting procedures and pay in money and kind for officers and crew.
15. Information about the sailing and navigation of ships in the 16th century.
16. Fighting tactics.

THE SPANISH ARMADA
AND ITS DEFEAT

Again, the factors in history are important. The children should understand why Spain attacked and why the year 1588 was chosen for the attack.

SOME OF THE REASONS FOR THE LAUNCH OF THE ARMADA

1. Philip II, King of Spain, felt deceived and humiliated.
2. England was a champion of Protestantism, Spain of Catholicism.
3. The Pope excommunicated Elizabeth I.
4. Piratical attacks on Spaniards - Drake's voyage (1585) and Elizabeth's confiscation of the treasure ship taking refuge in Falmouth harbour.
5. Elizabeth interfered in the Netherlands.
6. The death of Mary Stuart who was executed at Fotheringay Castle in 1587.
7. Philip was named as heir to Mary Stuart.
8. Spain helped Catholics in Ireland to rebel against England (1579).
9. Spain and France were at peace.
10. The Spanish failure to get Elizabeth assassinated (by helping in plots against the Queen).
11. Philip thought England was weak.
12. Philip thought it to be a crusade for the sake of Catholicism.

ATTACK AND DEFEAT The events shoud be carefully noted. There was an element of Spanish misman-agement in the attack. Briefly, Philip gathered together a large fleet of 130 ships. 30 of these were fighting ships, the other 100 carried stores, supplies and soldiers. In July, 1588 it set sail for the Netherlands to take another 20,000 soldiers on board and then planned to sail up the English Channel and land on the south coast of England. The Spanish Armada was led by the Duke of Medina Sidonia and this admiral was aboard the vessel, the *San Martin de Portugal*. Look-outs sighted the Spanish fleet and English ships commanded by Lord Howard and Sir Francis Drake (and with Frobisher and Hawkins) attacked the Armada on 21 July near Plymouth. Fierce battles were fought off the Isle of Wight and more English ships joined in the battle. Many heavy Spanish galleons were damaged and the Duke of Medina Sidonia ordered his fleet to drop anchor near Calais. During the night the English set alight 8 old English ships loaded with wood, barrels of tar and gunpowder and then sent them towards the Spanish fleet. These 'fire ships' caused havoc amongst the closely packed Spanish vessels and the Armada fled out to sea. There, the English were waiting for them. A naval battle lasting 8 hours ensued, several galleons were sunk and thousands of Spaniards killed. The English ships were smaller, faster and had more guns than the huge, cumbersome Spanish vessels. The English tried to drive the enemy ships on to sandbanks but the winds changed and the Spanish escaped to the open sea. The fleet sailing northward was now in tatters - broken masts, leaking, full of sick and wounded sailors and soldiers with food and water supplies running out. The fleet had to sail around the North of Scotland. There they ran into heavy gales and many were wrecked on the rocky coasts. Only 60 ships got back to Spain.

RESULTS included

1. Spain was humiliated. There were no further major attacks.
2. The English navy became stronger.
3. Elizabeth was regarded as a heroine at home.
4. The Reformation was made more secure.
5. Spanish power declined while English power grew greater.
6. England began to emerge as a European power.
7. England followed the defeat by acquisitions in the New World.

Discuss the development of the navy with the children. Discuss life at sea and compare it with conditions today. Children should be able to name the parts of a typical Tudor ship and know the elements of how naval warfare was conducted. The *Mary Rose* is most important and if possible children should not only know about this vessel but should be taken to Portsmouth on a visit. Discuss the problems of long sea voyages in Tudor times. Compare and contrast the Tudor navy with the modern navy. Role play can be used again - the feelings and reactions of an ordinary seaman, a captain or officer on one of the Tudor ships or a marine - a soldier aboard ready to fight when called upon. Also discuss eating habits and problems on board Tudor vessels. Outline the build-up and reasons for the Armada. Outline its defeat and discuss its importance. Give reasons for the attack and the results of its failure. Examine the roles of the monarchs in the build-up of English naval power and success.

THE COURSE OF THE SPANISH ARMADA

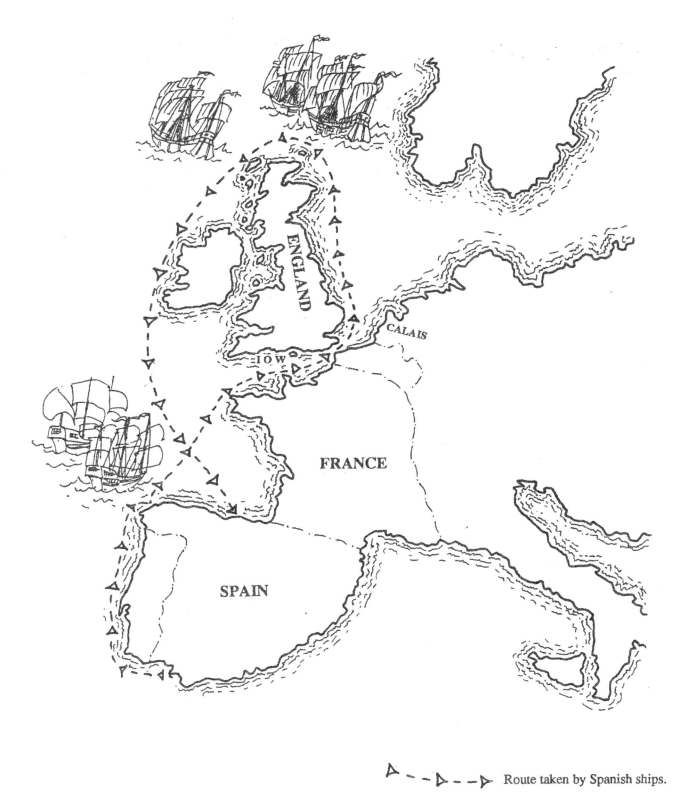

▷ - - ▷ - - ▷ Route taken by Spanish ships.

The Course of the Spanish Armada

WOMEN IN TUDOR TIMES

STATUS AND EDUCATION In Tudor times women were regarded as being subordinate to men but nevertheless they had a place of importance in society. The fact that the longest surviving monarch, Elizabeth I, was a woman helped their cause. Women did not receive the same education as men. Girls, like boys, were taught to read and write if facilities were available but girls did not attend grammar schools and were not allowed to go to university. Girls in wealthy families were taught at home by visiting tutors and learned music, dancing and French. Most girls from the lower classes were expected to help in the home and become good mothers and housewives.

CHILDBIRTH Generally, girls married young, between the age of 14 and 16. Childbirth was difficult especially as medical knowledge was so limited and many young women died giving birth. Even if the baby and mother survived, they might die soon after because of poor nursing care and lack of hygiene. Because of the risk of such early death, babies were always baptised as soon as possible. As soon as girls were out of baby clothes they were dressed like their mothers - little girls were regarded as adults in miniature.

BESS OF HARDWICK. Her records give an insight into the way a Tudor woman could progress in society. They show how she organised her daily life and the employment of her servants. Her father was an insignificant country gentlemen but eventually she became the countess of Shrewsbury. Married four times she became an astute merchant and prosperous farmer. Her household accounts showed she made shrewd deals involving cattle, pasture land and wool sales.

EVERYDAY LIFE OF A FARMER'S WIFE We can learn much about the wife of a farmer from *The Book of Husbandry* probably written by Sir Anthony Fitzherbert and first published in 1523. Her first duty was to wake up her husband but many more tasks were listed. She had to wake and dress the children, prepare her husband's breakfast, dinner and supper, and supervise the servants. She had to clean the house, feed the calves, prepare the milk, make butter and cheese, feed the pigs morning and evening, and have a care for the hens, ducks, and geese and collect their eggs. She was expected to put her husband's sheep to good use by making clothes from their wool, and know how to make hay, to winnow all kinds of corn, to make malt, and to help her *husband to fill the muck wain or dung cart*. She had to go to market if her husband was unable to go and be able to buy and sell shrewdly. She was expected to give a full and accurate account of all money she had spent and received and her husband was expected to do the same for her. Women worked hard in Tudor times.

GENERAL CHORES Homes had to be self sufficient and the necessary skills had to be acquired by women. Girls learned from their mothers how to cook and make meals, how to make jams and preserves and how to brew ale and beer and make wines and syrups from fruit, herbs and berries. They learned to stitch and sew and make clothes practising their stitches on samplers and embroidering cushions and pillows. They learned how to clean, card and dye wool and spin it into thread on a spinning wheel. They also had to learn to spin linen thread from flax. Some women wove thread into cloth. Women made candles for lighting. Keeping things clean was difficult. Soap made at home from fat and ashes and stored in a barrel was ineffective and unpleasant. Water was in short supply but clothes had to be washed and dried.

Discuss the position of women in Tudor society with the children. Compare and contrast with today. Explain how girls were educated and discuss the pitfalls of early marriages. Explain how the children of monarchs were betrothed in the cradle. Discuss the problems encountered by Tudor women. Let the children write an account of a day in the life of a Tudor housewife.

THE ENGLISH RENAISSANCE

First, it is necessary to explain the word *Renaissance* and then to show how it affected England and Scotland.

IN EUROPE The word Renaissance describes the new spirit which which was born in Europe during the 16th century. During the Middle Ages most people were content to believe something was true because it had always been said to be so. The new spirit was keenly critical and demanded reasons before anything would be believed. The Renaissance swept away false ideas and widened the outlook of people. This great movement spread more rapidly because of the invention of printing. It involved a revival of learning and art, religion and a physical world extended by vast geographical discoveries. There was also better understanding of the position of the earth in the solar system.

The movement is usually dated from the fall of Constantinople to the Turks in 1453 when the Greeks emigrated in great numbers to Italy and elsewhere taking with them the knowledge of Greek art, drama and learning which had been forgotten by Europe. Thus, Italy was the birth-place of the Renaissance. In the Church, it led to the Reformation, a fierce revolt against Papal pretensions and abuses in the Church.

IN ENGLAND in the days of Henry VIII the new learning was championed by the Oxford Reformers. Men like Dean Colet, Sir Thomas More, Thomas Linacre and William Grocyn replaced the study of logic and hide-bound theology by that of Greek and the best thought of the classical world. These men did not want violent revolt or change but hoped to revive old ideas with the new spirit. They did not wish to overturn the Church and set up a new one in its place. Sir Thomas More's *Utopia* describes a country where there are no aggressive wars, no religious persecution, no crime, no idleness, no overwork, no glaring contrasts of wealth and poverty. This would be a country where the worn-out social and economic system of the Middle Ages was replaced by a new and effective one based upon the Christian principles of brotherhood and toleration. Both Henry VIII and Wolsey were touched by the new spirit and did valuable work towards improving education in England.

Men like Luther and Calvin were leading a great religious reformation on the Continent. For some time England was untouched by these movements. However, when Henry VIII was trying to force the Pope to grant him a divorce from Catherine of Aragon, he was glad to seek the support of his subjects who, tired of the corrupt doctrines and practices of some of the clergy of the Catholic Church, supported the Protestant Reformation. Henry VIII dissociated himself from all Protestant doctrines by persecuting Protestant heretics. But his repudiation of Papal authority in the long run could only strengthen the hands of the Reformers and lead to the further religious changes which took place in the reign of his son, Edward VI, and the final Protestant settlement under Elizabeth.

IN SCOTLAND the new Renaissance spirit led to a complete religious reformation under the influence of Calvin. The changes came later than in England because Scotland was more isolated from Europe. In Scotland, the careless and worldly clergy had lost credibility with the people. Under the strong leadership of John Knox the flood of Protestantism overflowed the land. The Genevan form of Protestantism was set up under the name of Presbyterianism and the new sovereign, Mary Queen of Scots, was forced to accept what she did not have the power to alter. The Protestant reformation ended the Franco-Scottish alliance and made possible the later union of England and Scotland.

Make sure that the children know what the word *Renaissance* means. Start with rebirth which is an easy concept to understand. Explain why it was important - the revival of Galen in medicine for example - but often caused problems. Examine individual contributions, e.g. Henry VIII's patronage of Holbein (note the portraits he painted) and show how this led to the fulfilment of Elizabeth's time with especially drama (Shakespeare) and music (Byrd). Let the children make a list of new learning successes and show how this eventually helped scientific progress in the 17th century. Most important of all tell the children about the discovery of printing with movable type (by Johann Gutenberg in Germany c 1397 - 1468) and the first printing press set up by William Caxton in London in 1477. Examine the importance of the dissemination of information in printed books and what this did for reading and learning. Consider how this changed people's lives. Let them make their own printing blocks using potatoes or other materials. Let the children see how printing works. Compile biographies of leading Renaissance figures and discuss the Renaissance in the theatre mentioning Shakespeare and the Globe (especially the new replica of the Globe in Southwark).

THE NEW WORLD
AND VOYAGES OF DISCOVERY

By the early 16th century brave sailors from Spain and Portugal had found routes to what was then called the 'New World'. These were the lands of the West Indies, America and the Pacific. Others like Bartholomew Diaz (1486) and Vasco da Gama sailed around Africa. Da Gama reached Calicut in India (May 1498). By May 1520 Magellan had reached Patagonia and in March and April 1521 he had reached Guam, and the Philippines. By these dates also Hernando Cortes had arrived in Mexico and ten years later Francisco Pizarro had landed in Peru (1530). These early Spanish and Portuguese explorers need to be studied in some detail for children to know how far exploration had progressed when England became involved. It is a good idea to let groups of children investigate all the explorers mentioned above and then to talk about them before considering the English explorers.

ENGLISH EXPLORERS John Cabot was the first of these. (Actually Cabot was an immigrant Italian!) In 1497 he reached Nova Scotia in North America. His son, Sebastian, later explored Hudson Bay (1508) and the coast of Paraguay. In 1553 Willoughby and Chancellor sailed to Russia and in 1576 Frobisher explored the Hudson Strait. The most famous of all English privateers and explorers was Sir Francis Drake. Tell the story of his vessel, the *Golden Hind*, and how he circumnavigated the world. He was the first Englishman to do so and the voyage took him nearly three years. Finally, Lancaster set up a trading base on Java in the Indian Ocean two years before Elizabeth died (1601).

A WALL CHART Plot these famous journeys with the children using world maps, atlases and a globe. Follow the routes of the Spanish, Portuguese and English. Colour the routes and mark the discoveries on a large world map. Use this as a classroom chart.

DANGERS OF EXPLORATION Outline the problems of sailing such long distances in the 16th century - no maps, few instruments, the use of approximations and dead reckoning, the sun, the stars and the moon. Highlight the superstitions of Tudor sailors and the diseases they suffered.

Discuss the benefits of the voyages and the drawbacks (influx of gold and silver made prices rise). Compare and contrast the exploration then with the exploration of space today. Let the children trace and colour drawings of the *Golden Hind* and examine it thoroughly. Make comparisons between this tiny vessel and ships sailing these distances today. Let the children imagine they are Sir Francis Drake or one of his men and tell what happened to them. Let them make a scrap book entitled, *Famous Tudor Sailors*. Illustrate each page with drawings and pictures. They could also write a play about Sir Francis Drake and his adventures ending with his knighthood. If possible, let the children visit the docks at Portsmouth, the naval dockyard at Chatham and the National Maritime Museum at Greenwich for further material and interest.

Give some time to the consideration of new products that came from voyages to the New World. Start by examining food wrappers. Ask the children where the ingredients listed on them came from, e.g a Bounty coconut bar - coconut, sugar and chocolate are all imports. Consider the introduction of tobacco to this country and remember that many people were addicted by the end of the Tudor period.

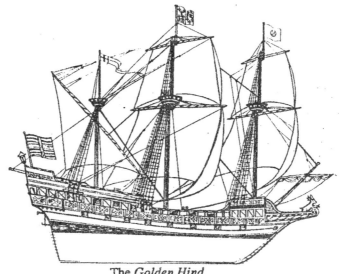

The *Golden Hind*

TUDOR PERSONALITIES

The Tudor period was the turning point between the Middle Ages and the beginning of modern times. Many people were involved in the changes that occurred at this time. Research into the lives of a few of these yields much about what it was like to live then. The study lends itself to role play. The following list is by no means exhaustive but contains several people worth looking at.

1. John Cabot, Italian sailor and explorer who settled in Bristol.
2. Desiderius Erasmus, Dutch scholar.
3. Dean Colet, English scholar.
4. Sir Thomas More, scholar, writer and statesman. Wrote *Utopia*.
5. Thomas Linacre, English scholar.
6. William Grocyn, English scholar.
7. Hans Holbein, famous German portrait painter.
8. Martin Luther, famous German religious reformer.
9. John Calvin, religious reformer.
10. John Knox, Scottish Protestant reformer.
11. William Cecil, statesman. Adviser to Elizabeth I.
12. Thomas Cranmer, Archbishop.
13. Thomas Cromwell, Lord Chancellor.
14. John Dee, famous astronomer.
15. Francis Drake, famous seaman. First to circumnavigate the world.
16. Robert Dudley, Earl of Leicester. One of Elizabeth's favourites.
17. Gerald Fitzgerald, famous Irish rebel.
18. Martin Frobisher, famous explorer.
19. Humphrey Gilbert, famous sailor. Discovered Newfoundland.
20. Thomas Gresham, important financier and banker.
21. Lady Jane Grey, Nine Days Queen.
22. Nicholas Hilliard, important portrait painter.
23. Hugh O'Neill, famous Irish leader.
24. Sir Walter Raleigh, explorer and privateer.
25. Edward Seymour, Duke of Somerset. Protector for Edward VI.
26. Duke of Northumberland. Protector for Edward VI.
27. Hugh Latimer, Bishop burnt at the stake.
28. Nicholas Ridley, Bishop burnt at the stake.
29. William Shakespeare, playwright.
30. Edmund Spencer, important poet.
31. Thomas Tallis, famous musician and composer.
32. William Byrd, famous musician and composer.
33. William Caxton, first printing press in England.
34. Johann Gutenberg, first printing press in Germany.
35. Francis Walsingham, statesman and spy-master.
36. Thomas Wolsey, statesman and Cardinal.
37. Francis Bacon, statesman and author.
38. Perkin Warbeck, Pretender to the throne.
39. Lambert Simnel, Pretender to the throne.
40. Richard Empson, statesman.
41. Edmund Dudley, statesman.
42. Stephen Gardiner, Bishop of Winchester.
43. William Cecil, Lord Burghley, Elizabethan statesman.
44. Sir Robert Dimock, King's champion.
45. Walter Rippon, coach-builder.
46. William Warham, Archbishop.
47. John Foxe, author - *Book of Martyrs*.
48. John Fisher, Bishop of Rochester.
49. William Tyndale, translator - Bible in English.
50. John Stubbs, author, Puritan propagandist.
51. Ralph Morice, biographer.
52. Humphrey Coke, master carpenter.
53. William Vertue, master builder.
54. Henry Redman, master builder.
55. James Needham, famous carpenter.
56. John Vesey, Bishop and philanthropist.
57. Elizabeth Talbot, Countess of Shrewsbury, famous Tudor lady.
58. Ben Jonson, playwright.
59. Jean Carré, glass manufacturer.
60 John Lennard, glass manufacturer.
61. John Hawkins, sailor and privateer.
62. Edmund Bonner, Bishop of London.
63. Sir Anthony Fitzherbert, author - *The book of Husbandry*.
64. Sir Thomas Elyot, courtier, diplomat and author.
65. John Kaye, famous Elizabethan doctor.
66. Lord Howard of Effingham, naval commander.
67. Sebastian Cabot, explorer.
68. Richard Chancellor, sailor, explorer.
69. Sir Hugh Willoughby, sailor, explorer.
70. Anthony Jenkinson, famous traveller.
71. Thomas Randolph, experienced diplomat.
72. John Stow, author, wrote about London.
73. Richard Hakluyt, Oxford scholar, author.
74. Thomas Cavendish, English sailor, explorer.
75. Duke of Parma, Spanish soldier, commanded troops in the Netherlands.
76. Duke of Medina Sidonia, Spaniard who commanded the Spanish Armada.
77. Sir Thomas Wyatt, diplomat, courtier and poet.
78. John Cheke, scholar, Professor of Civil Law.
79. Robert Devereux, Earl of Essex, statesman.
80. George Turbervile, writer and poet.
81. John Marbeck, composer and organist.
82. John Bale, playwright.
83. John Heywood, playwright.
84. Nicholas Udall, playwright.
85. Thomas Norton, playwright.
86. Thomas Sackville, playwright.
87. Christopher Marlowe, playwright.
88. Richard Burbage, actor.
89. Paul Hentzner, German traveller.
90. Miles Huggarde, poet. Also wrote anti-Protestant tracts.
91. Roger Ascham, scholar, writer.
92. William Coverdale, translator - 'The English Bible'.
93. William Harrison, travel writer.
94. Thomas Dekker, playwright.
95. Thomas Tusser, author - book on husbandry.
96. William Vaughan, author - *Delights for Ladies*.
97. Sir James Melville, courtier, author.
98. Anne Askew, Protestant sympathiser. Leading woman in Henry VIII's day.
99. Jean du Bellay, French ambassador in London.
100. Thomas Wyatt (the younger), rebel - Wyatt's rebellion.
101. Robert Kett, rebel - Kett's rebellion.
102. William Gilbert, famous physician.

ADDITIONAL TEACHING IDEAS
AND STRATEGIES
THE TUDORS

This book contains opportunities to give your pupils an insight into **historical concepts.** These embrace time, especially **chronological time:** the value of **historical evidence:** the **importance of changes,** especially on social life and **causes** and **results** of **historical movements.** Similarities and **differences** are also emphasized and the contributions of **individuals** to history are also important. Students need to learn **historical skills** and to sharpen these as they proceed with their studies. **Providing the evidence** is part of a teacher's work. Children have to learn to **interpret** this whether it is from original or secondary sources. They have to learn to make the appropriate **assumptions** and **deductions. Sequencing** and **observation** are also important historical skills. Students also have to learn how to **communicate** and **record** what they have learned.

Finally, they have to develop an enquiring mind. They need to know that there might be different attitudes to historical movements and developments. Also, history cannot be studied in a vacuum: geography, science, music, art, mathematics, technology and other specialisms have a bearing upon it. Students must learn that there are such things as conflicting evidence or inconclusive or incomplete evidence. They also have to develop a feeling for the past - an empathy if you like - which is often difficult to cultivate in the young child. It is hoped that these additional notes will help to do all this and to show that history has an extra-curricular aspect second to none.

DISCUSSION Techniques include question and answer; debate; stories in miniature; contrasts and similarities with today; a day in the life of a ...; using a film, tape or radio play to start the discussion; using a passage from Shakespeare, Ben Jonson or Christopher Marlowe to start discussion.

MATHEMATICS This is most relevant to places. Pose the questions on any Tudor building, place or object *What is it? What was it used for? How many were there? How old is it? When was it made or built? How much did it cost?* Begin with objects.

SCIENCE Science is concerned with asking questions and finding out. This is especially relevant to the historical environment. Again the questions *how? why?* and *when?* are relevant. As far as the Tudors are concerned, consider the influence of humans on the historic environment - scientific discoveries are important here. Consider Tudor diet, comparative diets. *What is a balanced diet? How did the Tudors fare?*

ROLE PLAY This can be used instead of reading or looking at material. Pupils take on the personality of people from the past. They can learn about a character, an event or a place: a Tudor girl or boy, a Tudor schoolroom, a Tudor school day, a Tudor mansion, servant, the squire and his lady, life in a Tudor home, a day in the life of a Tudor chimney sweep or a Tudor messenger or a day in the life of an apprentice.

USING PORTRAITS A portrait is a piece of work (painting, drawing or similar art-work) for which the subject consciously posed. Much can be learned from these but children need 'clues' and practice. Consider costume, colour, jewellery, armour and weapons. Other factors to consider are facial expression and pose, background and accessories. Begin with simple examples and a questionnaire. Queen Elizabeth alone is a good starting example for younger children.

STORY TELLING Young children love to be told a story. It is often a good idea to start or finish a lesson with a story. There are many books full of good stories and material. A visit to a historical site can be the basis for many stories.

USING TUDOR HOUSES/LISTED BUILDINGS A historic house is any building used in the past as a home or built for that purpose. They are still pictures of the past. Children can absorb the past. They can look at the size of the rooms, the kind and arrangement of furniture, where people cooked, ate and slept, discover the lives of those who lived upstairs and downstairs. Find out who looks after the building today. (See Visiting Historical Sites.)

LEARNING FROM OBJECTS Using these is a very important teaching strategy. Children need to examine the object if possible and note its physical features, how it was made, what it is made of, its functions, its design and value. Let them see Tudor objects (a good place to see them is at an exhibition like the *Mary Rose*). Domestic utensils are often very interesting and children marvel at how things were done.

USING WOODCUTS AND PRINTS Tudor prints were made by carving the picture into a piece of wood and then using the wood as a printing block. Find books with Tudor prints and use them in your classwork. Woodcuts are similar and many copies of these exist in books and manuscripts. Children can compare these prints and woodcuts with written evidence. Let them examine them through a magnifying glass. Turn this exercise into a game - hunting for evidence and asking the questions who? why? when? how? and where? Make 'potato cuts' from thick slices of peeled potatoes.

DRAMA Besides role play, drama is another useful teaching strategy. This can start as 'Tudor Characters', a kind of 'What's My Line' and finally a full dramatic scene. Here are some ideas.
  1. A Tudor court room with JPs and a vagrant. Create the atmosphere for the event - the children are performers and audience.
  2. A drama indoors. A Tudor episode in a nobleman's mansion with the family, servants, a cook, ladies' maids, other servants.
  3. A drama set in a Tudor schoolroom - strong armed teacher against disobedient children.
  4. A drama set on a Tudor warship. 5. A drama set in a Tudor village.
  6. A London scene. 7. A drama set in a master's house with apprentices.
  9. An interview with an important person who lived in Tudor times. If possible use a tape recorder or video camera.

USING GEOGRAPHY The factors of location, accessibility to raw materials and skilled people, the resources needed to manufacture goods and how the products were marketed are all important. Tudor industrial sites are interesting to study. Consider where and why particular industries flourished. The children need to mark them on a map and again ask *when? why? who? how?* Let them consider the problems of industrial growth. Pay particular attention to the growth of the woollen industry and the new industries of brick-making and glass making. The discoveries in the New World are important. Let the children plot these discoveries on a globe or atlas. Give them blank maps of the world and they can mark the routes on these. When complete they can stick them in their notebooks. Discuss imports and exports. Use food wrappers and the children should find out where the foods are grown: consider whether such products were available in Tudor times.

USING TOWN TRAILS Much that is Tudor is dead and gone. But there are still some Tudor buildings and houses about. Look at maps and guide books to try and find out where these are. A trip to Lavenham could prove rewarding. If you can visit something built or originating in Tudor times play 'I Spy Tudor'.

USING FAMILY AND DOMESTIC LIFE Discuss a typical Tudor family and compare and contrast with today's. Invent a Tudor family and get the children to draw a family tree. They can then draw their own family trees starting with grandparents and compare them. Compare and contrast family life in Tudor times with today. Use a 'Then' and 'Now' chart. Compare domestic arrangements. Illustrate with reference to servants, the aged and the young. Discuss the changes in housing - own bedroom, bathrooms, flush toilets, soap and water, toothpaste and so on. [It may be advisable to discuss a general Tudor family and a general family today rather than private details of the families of the children.]

USING DIET AND COOKING Use textbooks to discuss Tudor diets. Use old cookery books for Tudor recipes. Discuss how the poor fared and what Tudor children ate. Compare the foods of a farm labourer with that of a noble. Discuss the importance of the price of bread and fluctuating prices in Tudor times. Remember that water supply was a major Tudor problem. Discuss differences in cooking methods and the preservation of food. Discuss the problems of a society cooking without gas and electricity. Explain why virtually everything had to be made at home.

TUDOR PASTIMES AND ENTERTAINMENT Let the children research the details of these. Children might design a Tudor book or file cover for their work. Explain why there are difficulties with Tudor times such as few illustrations, no photographs but printing had been invented and there is evidence from prints. The children might write short pieces of prose on 'Life in a Tudor Village' (or town) or 'Life in a Tudor School'. A child could pretend to be a journalist and write an article, e.g. on 'The Loss of the *Mary Rose*'.

The Tudors made their own entertainment. Compare with the situation today. Play Tudor games with the children. Remember that many of our nursery rhymes go back to Tudor ballads - Tom thumb, Mother Hubbard, Jack Spratt, Margery Daw and Little Tommy Tucker are a few.

Photocopy some famous scenes from books and get the children to act out the various roles and events - the knighting of Francis Drake, Sir Walter Raleigh and his cloak, the execution of Mary Stuart and the imprisonment of Lady Jane Grey. It is more fun if the children dress up.

A NOTE ON THE PUPILS' WORKSHEETS The worksheets are designed for use in class and can be adapted as the teacher wishes. Questions after a diagram or print may be answered ORALLY or in WRITING.

VISITING HISTORICAL SITES

THE IMPORTANCE OF VISITS

A visit to a Tudor site or a museum brings the threads of the study together. 'Chalk and talk' are now turned into reality. Pupils can see for themselves where the Tudors lived and 'seeing is believing'. Observation is the keynote but there may be possibilities of participation in the Tudor way of life and in role play. Fortunately, throughout Britain there are many Tudor sites and excellent museum displays. Try to visit the chosen site alone before taking a group or class.

PREPARATION FOR A SITE VISIT

BEFORE THE VISIT

Choose a site that is appropriate and can be easily reached or preferably is near to the school. Make a list of the reasons for and the aims of the visit. Decide which National Curriculum topics are to be covered and which targets you wish to meet. If possible visit the site yourself before you take the class. Most sites have teachers' notes and worksheets which are usually helpful and save a great deal of time. You may wish to modify them to suit your class and your own objectives. It is very important to prepare the children for the visit. The site will seem exciting and strange to them when they arrive. They may wander off aimlessly, waste time and possibly get into dangerous situations.

Decide what you are going to tell the children about the site before the visit. Few are likely to be born historians and they need enough information to enable them to understand what they will see during the visit. Slides, photographs, ground/site plans are helpful beforehand if they are available. It may be useful to talk about Tudor sites in general and then discuss the site you are planning to visit in particular. One visit is not going to cover everything and so decide exactly what you want to concentrate on. Depending on the age and abilities of the children, keep it short and keep it simple. Above all, they should enjoy it educationally and socially.

It may be necessary to enhance the children's visual skills. The visit may involve using the following skills at some level.

1. Observation skills.
2. Recording skills.
3. Being able to make comparisons.
4. Being able to make deductions.
5. Reading, writing and comprehension skills.
6. Measuring skills.
7. Estimating skills.
8. The ability to read maps.
9. The ability to read plans.
10. Mathematical skills.
11. Scientific skills.
12. Social skills, especially sharing and communicating.

A sense of time may be learned from the site and youngsters may realise the importance of historical evidence. Aesthetically, the group may gain a great deal from what they see. Pupils need guidance about the information and data they can gather at the site. Practise by organising a survey of the school, school grounds, village or an area of a town before the visit. This should be simple but it is helpful to observe a familiar place closely and discover the relationship between information on a flat piece of paper like a map or diagram drawn by the pupil and the 3D environment.

Devise your own activity pack for use on the site. This should include illustrations, a questionnaire and questions requiring observation and deduction.

TEACHERS' CHECK LIST

On your personal visit before taking your group or class consider the following.

1. Kind of site. Is the site industrial, commercial, residential or other? Is the building decorative or utilitarian or both? If residential, was it the home of wealthy or poor Tudors?

2. Geography of the land. Consider this, the lie of the land and the geology of the site.

3. Location of the site. Why was the site chosen? Does the location have any advantages?

4. Previous occupation of the site. Was the site occupied before Tudor times? If so, how did the Tudors change or adapt it?

5. Changes in the site. Has the site been changed or affected by 'modern' developments such as the building of a motorway or housing? If so, what did it look like in Tudor times?

6. Discoveries. Have there been any important discoveries or finds at the site? If so, pinpoint them so that you can discuss them with the children.

7. When was the site used? Was it used in peacetime or wartime or both?

8. Buildings. Consider the buildings. What kinds of homes were they, what was their size and where were they located?

9. Size of the community. Consider the size and social structure of the community associated with the site. Did any important people live in the community? Are there any indications of a farrier, doctor, lawyer, school teacher … ? Is an author or poet connected with the area?

10. Occupation. What was the occupation of the owner - landowner, mine owner, aristocrat, sailor …?

11. Food. What evidence is there about diet, cooking and cooking utensils? What can be learned about the storage and preparation of food in Tudor times? What size is the kitchen? How is it equipped?

12. Animals. Were animals such as horses or dogs kept on the site?

13. Meat. Is there any evidence of food processing, meat eating or meat cooking?

14. Food preservation. Are there any details of the storage of grain. Was food preserved?

15. Natural resources. What were the natural resources of the site - such as wood, stone, clay or charcoal? Were there any natural resources close by? Have these been exhausted?

16. Skilled work. Is there any evidence of skilled work such as making cloth, leather goods … ? Were the rooms planned and furnished by someone important? Are the rooms (and the building) finely decorated, e.g. with expensive wood panelling or gold leaf?

17. Grounds. Are the grounds extensive and well laid out? Who planned them and who maintains them now?

18. Metal working. Is there any evidence of metal working (lead, tin, bronze, iron, silver, gold) at the site? Look for equipment, tools, jewellery and artefacts.

19. Other materials. Is there any evidence of the use of stone, shale, slate or other materials on the site? (If so have they been used practically or aesthetically or both?

20. Clothes. Is there any evidence of the production of woollen or linen material and clothes?

21. Women. What did the women do? How do you know?

22. Finds of special interest.

SOME PLACES TO VISIT

Here are some museums, houses and places of Tudor interest to visit. Of particular interest is the *Mary Rose* situated in Portsmouth Docks. We have prepared a special activity pack on this vessel for the *Mary Rose* Trust which is available from the Trustees.

Adlington Hall, Cheshire.

Anne Hathaway's Cottage, Stratford-upon-Avon.

Arreton Manor, Isle fo Wight.

Arundel Castle, West Sussex.

Baddesley Clinton, Warwickshire.

Barrington Court, Somerset.

Benthall Hall, Shropshire.

Berkeley Castle, Gloucestershire.

Berwick-on-Tweed, Tudor castle and town walls.

Benthall Hall, Shropshire.

Bramhall Hall, Greater Manchester.

British Museum, London.

Broughton Castle, Oxfordshire.

Buckland Abbey, Devon.

Burghley House, Cambridgeshire.

Castle Acre Priory, Norfolk.

Charlecote Park, Warwickshire.

City Museum, Plymouth.

Cotehele House, St. Dominick, Cornwall.

Coughton Court, Warwickshire.

Elizabethan House, Plymouth.

Fountains Abbey, Yorkshire.

Geoffrey Museum, London..

Glastonbury Abbey, Somerset.

GLOBE THEATRE, London. Rebuilt replica of Shakespeare's theatre.

Hampton Court Palace, London.

Hardwick Hall, Derbyshire.

Hever Castle, Kent.

Holyrood Palace, Edinburgh.

Igtham Mote, Kent.

Jesus College, Oxford.

Knole, Kent.

Lacock Abbey, Wiltshire.

Little Moreton Hall, Cheshire.

Llancaiach Fawr, Nelson, Mid Glamorganshire.

London Museum.

Longleat, Wiltshire.

Lyveden New Bield, Northamptonshire.

MARY ROSE, Portsmouth.

Merchant's House, Plymouth.

Melford Hall, Suffolk.

Montecute House, Somerset.

Moseley Old Hall, Staffordshire.

Mottisfont Abbey, Hampshire.

Museum of London, London Wall.

National Maritime Museum, Greenwich.

National Portrait Gallery, London.

Nummington Hall, North Yorkshire.

Ormondes Castle, Tipperary, Eire.

Oxburgh Hall, Norfolk.

Paycocke's, Essex.

Penshurst Place, Kent

The Red Lodge, Bristol.

Rievaulx Abbey, Yorkshire.

Speke Hall, Merseyside.

Stratford-on-Avon, Shakespeare's birthplace.

Sudeley Castle, Sudeley.

Sutton House, London.

Temple Newsam House, Leeds.

Tintern Abbey, Gwent.

Tower of London.

Trerice, Cornwall

Tudor Merchant's House, Tenby.

Ty Mawr, Gwynedd.

The Vyne, Hampshire.

Warwick Castle, Warwickshire.

Westminster Abbey, London.

West Stow Hall, Sussex.

Woburn Abbey, Befordshire.

Wollaton Hall, Nottinghamshire.

Yarmouth Castle, Isle of Wight.

AT THE SITE

Make use of the surroundings of the site as well as buildings there. Let the pupils study their surroundings including flora, fauna, trees (include bark rubbings if appropriate), animal habitats and so on. Instead of or as well as the guidance from activity sheets, the children may be asked to solve a problem from the past. Examples are:

You are administrator of this Tudor house. How would you preserve what is there?

Show how this house was organised in Tudor times.

A group of foreign tourists who have no previous knowledge of Tudor buildings intends to visit the place. List the main features you would tell them about. Why have you chosen these features?

The children may imagine they are Tudors at the site. Give them roles to play and work out how these roles may be fulfilled. If it is practical, pupils can wear Tudor dress and the site can be used to re-enact an event from history such as the birth of Henry VII or the preparations for a visit by Elizabeth I. The use of an unfamiliar site in this way may be difficult and not as useful as using role play as part of the follow up.

FOLLOW UP TO A VISIT

To reinforce the visit you might consider the following when you return to the classroom.

1. Devise a quiz to find out how much the children have learned.
2. Devise other written work especially making them see the site as a place where people lived and worked. How did the site operate on a daily basis? Use actual characters from Tudor times if possible.
3. Guide the children to write reports on particular aspects of the site - the Tudor kitchen, the Tudor Long Gallery and so on.
4. Use the activity pack/worksheets/guide book.
5. Organise the pupils to make a display of any written work - drawings, maps, ground plans, photographs … Develop this for use in the classroom and classify and label any objects. Some children may make models, (some accurately scaled) costumed figures and measured drawings.
6. Pinpoint any technology from the site such as roads, buildings or statues. Spinning, dyeing, weaving and artefacts are part of this.
7. Pinpoint the diet and ways in which food was cooked.
8. Pupils could make a frieze or collage. Brass or other rubbings may be possible.
9. The pupils could write and act a play or situation which might have occurred on the site such as a conversation between a Tudor servant and his/her master.
10. Use slides, drawings, photographs and so on to prepare an audio-visual presentation. Tape-slide sequences, presentations or a video presentation may be possible depending on the site and the age and abilities of the children.
11. Pupils may examine documents (i.e. copies of documents) from the site. They could ask themselves

    When was it written?   How do we know when it was written?
    Who wrote it?   Why was it written?
    What sort of document is it? (Personal communication, order or command, official or unofficial …)
    Are there any differences between this document and others? Compare and contrast the documents if more than one is available.
    Is it one of a series of documents?   How do we know the original is genuine?

Finally, it is necessary to evaluate the visit objectively and write a brief report on how such a visit may be improved next time.

BOOKLIST / RESOURCES

GENERAL REFERENCE BOOKS/PUBLICATIONS

Bindoff, S.T.,	*Tudor England*, Penguin, 1951
Black, J.B.,	*The Reign of Elizabeth*, OUP, 2nd. ed., 1959
Briggs, A.,	*A Social History of England*, Weidenfeld and Nicolson, 1983
Brown, J.R.,	*Shakespeare and His Theatre*, Kestrel Books, 1982
Cartwright, F.F.,	*A Social History of Medicine*, Longman, 1977
Clout, H.	*The Times, London History Atlas*, Times Books, 1991
Fraser, A.,	*Mary Queen of Scots*, Methuen, 1970
Harrison, G.B.,	*The Letters of Queen Elizabeth*, Cassell, 1935
Hartley, D.,	*Food in England*, Macdonald and Jane's, 1954
Hurstfield, J. and Smith, A.G., (eds.),	*Elizabethan People, State and Society*, (Documents), Edward Arnold, 1972
Lacey, R.,	*The Life and Times of Henry VIII*, Book Club Associates, 1972
Lewis, M.,	*The History of the British Navy*, Penguin Books, 1957
Lockyer, R.,	*Tudor and Stuart Britain, 1471 - 1714*, Longman, 1964
Mackie, J.D.,	*The Earlier Tudors*, OUP, 1959
Neale, J.E.,	*Queen Elizabeth I*, Penguin, 1960
Plumb, J.H. and Wheldon, H.,	*Royal Heritage*, Chancellor Press, 1984
Ridley, J.,	*The Tudor Age*, Guild Publishing, 1988
Smurthwaite, D.,	*The Complete Guide to the Battlefields of Britain*, Penguin, 1984
Sitwell, E.,	*The Queens and the Hive*, World Books, 1962
Steward, R.,	*The Illustrated Almanac of Historical Facts*, Prentice Hall, 1992
Williams, N.,	*The Life and Times of Elizabeth I*, Book Club Associates, 1972

Tudor Writers (For Children) Any Edition

Bailey, D.,	*Tudors*, Hodder and Stoughton, 1993
Clements, G.,	*The Picture History of Great Inventors*, Studio Editions, 1995
Gerrard, R.,	*Sir Francis Drake: his daring deeds*, Gollancz, 1988
Harnett, C.,	*The Woolpack*, Penguin, 1989
Honey, A.,	*Investigating the Tudors*, National Trust Enterprises, 1993
Jessup, J.,	*Tudor Towns*, Wayland, 1990
Langley, A.,	*The Tudors, 1485 - 1603*, Hamlyn, 1993
Trease, G.,	*Cue for Treason*, Penguin, 1989
Uttley, A.,	*Traveller in Time*, Penguin, 1977

SEE ALSO
Unstead R.H., *Tudors and Stuarts*, A & C Black, 1991
The Tudors, Living History Series, Wayland, 1990
Tudor Britain, Living History Series, Wayland, 1991
Tudor Sailors, Living History Series, Wayland, 1991

ACTIVITY PACKS We have published a number of children's Activity Packs on this period.
The Tudors
Henry VIII
Elizabeth I
The *Mary Rose*.
Houses of Parliament
Separate Packs, Domino Books (Wales) Ltd., 1996.

ORIGINAL SOURCES
Besides the source books mentioned in the general list above, teachers are advised to consult parliamentary papers and Acts published throughout the period. Parish Records can also be useful for they give details of baptisms, marriages and burials. John Stow's *Survey of London* (1598) gives information about London in Tudor times and *The Letters of Queen Elizabeth* (ed. G.B. Harrison) is a useful source for Elizabethan England. Teachers are also advised to look out for useful material when they take children on school visits. One fascinating book from Portsmouth is *The 'Mary Rose'*, a guide to the exhibition and ship, published by the *Mary Rose* Trust. Do not forget our Activity Pack on the ship which we researched and published for the *Mary Rose* Trust.

THE TUDOR MONARCHS - GENEALOGICAL TABLE

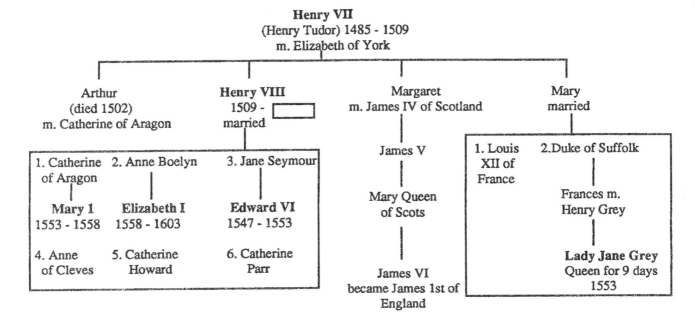

Use this Tudor family tree to answer these questions.

1. How many Tudor monarchs were there? Make a chronological list of them.

2. Are the dates in the table birth or death dates? If not what are they?

3. Work out the date that is missing for Henry VIII.

4. Which Tudor monarch ruled
   (a) for the shortest time,
   (b) for the longest time?

5. Which Tudor monarchs had
   (a) most wives or husbands,
   (b) did not marry at all,
   (c) had most children?

6. Who was the mother of
   (a) Mary Tudor,
   (b) Edward VI,
   (c) Elizabeth I?

7. Which queen reigned for just 9 days?

8. 'Henry VIII married his sister-in-law.' True or false? Give a reason for your answer.

9. Which daughter of Henry VII eventually led to the Stuart line?

10. Why was the marriage of Henry VII to Elizabeth of York so important?

I AM KING

Henry VII being crowned King.

Henry VII was crowned King immediately after he had defeated Richard III at the Battle of Bosworth Field in 1485. He then sent men to fetch Elizabeth of York from Sheriffhutton while he marched to London. In the capital he summoned a Parliament which passed an Act declaring that he was the rightful King of England.

Imagine you are Henry VII.

1. What would you do to make sure your reign continued?
    What did Henry VII do?

2. How would you make yourself a strong king?
    What did Henry VII do?

3. If you were opposed by others who said they should have the throne what would you do?
    What did Henry VII do?

4. Who were the Pretenders?

5. You are a reporter on the *Daily Argus* and have been commissioned to write an eye witness account of the Battle of Bosworth Field. What would you write?
    [Begin
    I am at Bosworth Field ...
    and remember to write about the crowning of the new king.]

PRIMARY AND SECONDARY SOURCES

Read the following passages and then answer the questions that follow them.

PASSAGE A

London, a place both for the beauty of buildings, infinite riches, variety of all things that excelleth, all the cities in the world, in so much that it may be called the storehouse and mart of all Europe ... What can there be in any place under the heavens that is not in this noble city either to be bought or borrowed?

It hath divers hospitals for the relieving of the poor, six score fair churches for divine service, a glorious bourse which they call the Royal Exchange, for the meeting of merchants of all countries where any traffic is to be had. Among all the strange and beautiful shows me thinketh there is none so notable as the bridge which crosseth the Thames.

John Lyly, Euphues and his England, 1581

PASSAGE B

When Henry VII's army reached London in September 1485 after their victory at Bosworth, a hitherto unknown illness appeared, which became known as 'the sweating sickness', or 'the sweat'. It forced Henry VII to postpone his coronation till 30 October. This outbreak passed away quite quickly, but the sweating sickness returned from time to time, and with particular virulence in 1517, 1528 and 1551. In July 1517, four hundred people died in Oxford in one week; in some towns, one third or even half of the inhabitants died. In 1528, two thousand died in London; and in July 1551, eight hundred died in London in a week.

The disease came on very suddenly. People who were feeling perfectly well were suddenly affected as they lay in bed, sat at the dinner table, or walked in the street. They sweated profusely, and were dead, sometimes within ten or twelve hours, and sometimes within four hours; *some merry at dinner, and dead at supper*, wrote the Tudor historian, Edward Hall. If they survived for twenty-four hours they were saved, and recovered very quickly. It was important that the patient should be neither too hot nor too cold; he should lie quietly in bed, well wrapped in warm blankets but in a room which was only moderately warm, with his arms crossed on his breast, in order to prevent the air from reaching his armpits. Although his fever made him very thirsty, it was important that he should not be given a cold drink, for those who drank anything always died. Women were much less likely to catch the sweat than men, though Henry VIII was being over-confident when he believed during the epidemic of 1528 that Anne Boleyn would escape the infection which had appeared in her household; she caught the sweat, but quickly recovered.

From *The Tudor Age* by Jasper Ridley , pages 248 - 249. Published by Guild Publishing, 1988.

1. Which of the passages A and B may be described as a primary source? Give a reason for your answer.

2 Which of the passages above is a secondary source? What do you understand by a secondary source?

3. Pick three words from the passages above which would not be used today and which might be called 'old' English.

These questions are on Passage B only.

4. What was the disease called? Give a modern name for it.

5. Give three main dates in the Tudor period when it broke out?

6. Describe the symptoms of the disease.

7. Who were more likely to catch the disease, men or women?

8. What were the attitudes of Henry VII and Henry VIII to the disease?

9. What future Queen caught the disease in 1528 and how did it affect her?

10. How did the Tudors treat patients who had the illness?

11. Name one other disease from which many people died that re-ocurred during Tudor times.

12. Why did the Tudors find it difficult to deal with serious illness?

SCHOOL IN TUDOR TIMES

The Tudor print below, dated about 1580, tells us us a lot about a typical 16th century grammar school. Look at the print then answer the questions that follow it.

1. Were there separate classes in Tudor times with their own teachers?

2. Did Tudor children learn music? How do you know?

3. Did Tudor children use printed books? How do you know?

4. Did the Tudors use wall charts and other visual aids? How do you know?

5. Can you see any evidence of misbehaviour in the picture?

6. How is a boy being punished in the picture?

7. Today, we speak of the 3Rs - reading, writing and arithmetic.
   Can you see evidence of these subjects being taught in the picture?

8. Were the children taught standing up or sitting down?

9. Are there any school desks in the print?

10. What is this object?
    Can you see someone using one in the picture?

11. Is anyone in the picture using a pencil?

12. How was ink made in Tudor times?

13. What is this object?
    Why did it become less important in Tudor times?

14. How were prints made in Tudor times?

HENRY VIII AND HIS SIX WIVES

Catherine of Aragon
1485 - 1536
married 1509,

Anne Boleyn
1502 - 1536
married 1532/3,

Jane Seymour
1509 - 1537
married 1536,

Anne of Cleves
1515 - 1557
married 1540,

Catherine Howard
1521 - 1542
married 1540,

Catherine Parr
1512 - 1548
married 1543,

Write what happened to each of Henry VIII's wives in the spaces underneath the pictures. Choose from: beheaded, died, divorced or outlived him.

The following extracts were written by people who knew Henry VIII when he was the new young monarch.

(a) The new king 'is extremely fond of tennis, at which game it is the prettiest sight in the world to see him play, his fair skin glowing through a shirt of the finest texture …'

(b) He was the 'handsomest potentate I ever set eyes upon: above the usual height, with an extremely fine calf to his leg, his complexion very fair and light, with auburn hair … and a round face so very beautiful that it would become a pretty woman …'

1. Are these extracts an original (primary) source or a secondary source?

2. Use the extracts to write a description of Henry VIII. Say if he liked sport and if he dressed well. Say whether he was tall or short, good looking or ugly and so on.

3. Look at a picture or painting of Henry VIII at the end of his reign? Why do you think his appearance had changed so much?

CLOSING THE MONASTERIES

1. Before the monasteries could be closed investigators were sent to find out all about them. This drawing shows one of the investigators at a monastery.
   Suggest five questions the investigator might ask and what the monks might say in reply.

2. Imagine you are a monk. Write an account of your day in the monastery.

3. Which of the following institutions were closed by Henry VIII - monasteries, nunneries, chapels, monastic schools and hospitals?

4. Give five reasons why Henry VIII decided to close the monasteries.

5. Give five effects the closure of the monasteries had on the lives of local people.

6. Imagine you are a prioress in charge of a nunnery which is to be closed.
   Write a short paragraph saying how you feel about this.

7. Mime the following short scene without using any words:
   You are taking away ornaments from a monastery in Norfolk. They are heavy to carry but with some effort you manage. Two monks are trying to stop you but you push them away. By the side of the footpath leading to the abbey, three young monks are crying. One is very upset and is waving a piece of paper, a protest against your actions. You ignore them and organise your fellow workers to remove more items from the monastery. How will the scene end?

THE BOY KING - EDWARD VI

Edward was only nine years old when he came to throne in 1547 and he died in July, 1553 at the early age of 15. He was so young that Regents or Protectors were appointed to rule for him. The first was Protector Somerset (1547 - 49), then the Earl of Warwick, Protector Northumberland (1549 - 53).

1. During the time Edward was king, England became more Protestant. Give five changes which took place that helped the Protestant religion.

This letter was written by Edward VI when he was only twelve and a half years old. Answer the questions that follow it.

This yere of our Lord 1537, was a prince born to king Harry th' eight, by Jane Seymour, when quene, who w'in few days after the Birth of her soone died, and was buried at the castel of Windwore. This child was christened by the duke of Northfolke, the duke of Southfolke, and the archbishop of Caunterbury. Afterward was brought up till he came to six yeres old among the women. At the sixt yere of his age, he was brought up in learning by Mr. Doctour Cox who was after his amner [almoner], and Jhon cheke, Mr. of Arts, tow wel learned men, who sought to bring him up in learning of toungues, of the scripture of philosopie, and all liberal sciences. Also John Belmaine frenchman did teach him the french language. The 10 yere not yet ended, it was apointed he should be created prince of Wales, Duke of Cornwal, and Conte Palatine of Chester. At wich time , being the year of our L. 1547 the said king died of a dropsie as it was thought. After whos death incontinent came Edward erle of Hartford, and S. Antony Brown, Mr. of the horse, to convey this prince to Enfild, where the earle of Hertford declared to him and his younger Sister Elizabeth, the death of their father.

2. Is this a primary or secondary source? Give a reason for your answer.
3. Who was the prince in the letter?
4. Who was his younger sister? What did she become?
5. Who were his parents and what happened to his mother soon after his birth?
6. Who christened the young prince?
7. Who looked after the prince until he was six years old?
8. Name the men who taught the prince after he was six. What did they teach him?
9. Give the meaning of 'learning of tongues' and 'yere of our L.'
10. When did the father of the prince die?
11. Write out the letter using today's spelling and punctuation instead of the prince's.

Colour this drawing of Prince Edward VI. He had light brown hair. His cap is red velvet with a white feather. He is wearing a pink doublet, pink lower sleeves, a crimson coat with a white ermine fur lining and collar, gold lace on puffed sleeves edged with pearls, white stockings and crimson shoes.

MARY TUDOR - A CATHOLIC QUEEN

Mary Tudor reigned from 1553 - 58. During this time she wanted to make England a Catholic country again and many Protestants were burned at the stake. Look at the drawing below and then answer the questions below it.

1. This drawing shows the burning of Bishops Latimer and Ridley at the stake at Oxford. They were burned for 'heresy' and because of their deaths became 'martyrs'. Expain the meaning of heresy and martyr.

2. Why did Mary have people burned at the stake? What did people think happened to a victim's soul after the body had been burned?

3. The following events occurred as Mary tried to restore the Catholic faith to England. Fit them into a time-line showing when each happened.

Events

Six Articles Restored.

Latin Mass Restored.

Monasteries still in the possession of the Crown restored.

Thomas Cranmer, Archbishop of Canterbury, burned at the stake at Oxford.

Re-union of the Church of England with the Church of Rome.

Use of the English Prayer Book forbidden.

Foreign Protestant Preachers exiled.

Married Priests to separate from their wives.

Mary married Philip II of Spain.

Repeal of the Act of Supremacy.

Cardinal Pole became Papal Legate in England.

The Burning of Protestants began.

Catholic Mass Restored.

Use these dates for the Time - Line

1553

1554

1555

1556

THE NINE DAYS' QUEEN

These drawings tell the story of Lady Jane Grey who was Queen for just nine days. The first picture (A) shows Edward VI dying and the Duke of Northumberland reading the King's will. The other drawings are in the wrong order. Cut them out and paste them in the correct order and write captions for them. Then answer the following questions.

1. In what year did these events take place and how old was Lady Jane Grey?

2. What relation was Lady Jane Grey to
   (a) Edward VI and (b) the Duke of Northumberland?

3. Give two reasons why the Duke of Northumberland wanted Lady Jane Grey to be Queen.

4. What did the will of Edward VI say about who should succeed him?

5. Was the conspiracy successful? What happened to the conspirators and Lady Jane Grey? Who was eventually crowned as Queen?

6. Pretend you are a guard at the Tower of London. Write a letter to a friend telling him or her all you saw and heard about these events.

A

Edward VI is dying and
Northumberland is reading
the King's will.

B

C

D

THE VIRGIN QUEEN
ELIZABETH I

We can learn a great deal about this Tudor Queen from what she said and wrote. Look at the following extracts and then answer the questions that follow them.

A. Part of a poem written by Elizabeth.

I grieve and dare not show my
  discontent,
I love and yet am forced to
  seem to hate,
I do, yet dare not say I ever
  meant,
I seem start mute but inwardly
  do prate.
    I am and not, I freeze and
      yet am burned,
    Since from myself another
      self turned.

B. Elizabeth wrote this on the eve of the Armada.

For my part, I doubt no whit but that all this tyrannical, proud and brainsick attempt will be the beginning, though not the end, of the ruin of that King (Philip of Spain), *that most unkingly, even in the midst of treating peace, begins this wrongful war.*

C. Elizabeth said this on the eve of the Armada.

I know I have the Body but of a weak and feeble Woman, but I have the Heart and Stomach of a King, and of a King of England, too, and think foul Scorn that any Prince of Europe should dare to invade the Borders of my Realm. I my-self will take up arms.

D. Letter to the Earl of Essex dated 14 September, 1599.

You have possessed us with expectation that you would proceed as we have directed you, but your actions always show the contrary. To so perform the Ulster wars, if sickness of the army be the reason, why was not the action undertaken when the army was in better state? If winter's approach, why were the summer months of July and August lost? If the spring were too soon, and the summer followed otherwise spent, if the harvest that succeeded were so neglected as nothing hath been done, we must conclude that none of the four quarters of the year will be in season for you. Further we require you to consider whether we have not a great cause to think that your purpose is not to end the war. The state of every province of Ireland you describe to be in worse conditions than ever they were before you put foot in that kingdom.

Elizabeth R

1. Are these extracts primary or secondary sources?

2. From reading extract A which of the following do you think are true of Elizabeth?
   (a) She could do and say what she liked.   (b) She was hypocritical.
   (c) She was diplomatic.   (d) She was shrewd.
   (e) She had to be careful about what she said and did.

3. Give the meanings of *discontent, mute, inwardly, prate.*

4. What does extract B tell you about Elizabeth's attitude to Philip of Spain?
   Give the meanings of *brainsick, ruin, unkingly, treating peace, wrongful.*

5. Were her predictions about Philip's *ruin* correct? How do you know?

6. What does extract C tell you about Elizabeth?

7. What *Prince of Europe* was in Elizabeth's mind?

8. In extract D, Elizabeth is at her best: she is logical and sarcastic.
   What does she want Essex to do? What reasons does she suggest for his failure?
   What happened to Essex?

9. Elizabeth I is regarded as a great queen. Outline the things about her character that helped her to be great and keep control during her reign.

10. What does the R in Elizabeth's signature mean?

THE DEATH OF A QUEEN

Below is a portrait of Mary, Queen of Scots. A beauty, she had a full but troublesome life. Answer the questions that follow her portrait.

1. When and where was Mary born?

2. When was Mary crowned Queen of Scotland?

3. Name the man Mary married in 1558. How long did this first marriage last?

4. Complete the following genealogical table with reference to Mary Queen of Scots.

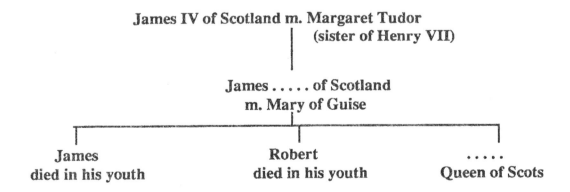

James IV of Scotland m. Margaret Tudor
(sister of Henry VII)

James . . . . . of Scotland
m. Mary of Guise

| James | Robert | . . . . . |
| died in his youth | died in his youth | Queen of Scots |

5. What does this genealogical table tell you about Mary's claim to the English throne?

6. Give an account of Mary's life after she returned to Scotland in 1561.

7. Name at least one plot to dethrone Elizabeth and put Mary on the throne.

8. Who signed Mary's death warrant and when?

9. When and where was Mary, Queen of Scots, executed?

TUDOR APPRENTICES

This drawing shows an apprentice at work in Tudor times.

1. What were apprentices?

2. What is the apprentice in the drawing doing?

3. The following is taken from his diary. Suppose you are the apprentice and write an account of your day.

6 am	Rise. Wake my master.
6.10 am	Breakfast.
6.30 am	Start work.
9 am	Make copies of master's correspondence.
9.30 am	Pack goods ready for despatch.
10.30 am	Watch goods are loaded on a ship.
11.30 am	Back at work learning my trade.
7 pm	Finish work.
	Quarrelled with another apprentice. Fought him.
9 pm	Returned to master's house just as the curfew bell struck 9 pm.

(a) What correspondence would you be copying?
(b) What goods would you be packing?
(c) Why would these goods be loaded on to a ship?

4. What was the curfew bell and why was it needed?

5. Before a master took a boy as an apprentice, an agreement was made and a sum of money exchanged hands.
(a) Name the agreement.
(b) How long did these agreements last in Tudor times?
(c) What did the master agree to?
(d) What did the apprentice promise?
(e) What was the sum of money called and who paid it?

WORK AND WORKERS IN TUDOR TIMES

The names of these people are linked to their work. Write the names and what they did under the pictures. Choose from: town crier (bellman), printer, rat catcher, bear minder, sweep, tinder box man, water carrier, court jester, candle-maker, archer.

Write ten occupations common today that would not have existed in Tudor times.

THE COUNTRYSIDE
LIFE IN A TUDOR VILLAGE

In Tudor times most people lived and worked in small villages in the countryside. In a typical village there were (a) a rich landlord, (b) some rich farmers who owned their land, (c) yeomen farmers who rented their farms from (a) or (b) and (d) husbandmen - farm labourers who worked the land but did not own or rent it. The villagers owned some strips of land around the village in common (i.e. they all owned it). Look at the drawing below and then answer the questions that follow.

A Tudor Village

1. Where did most people in a village work?
2. What do you understand by 'common' land? Mark the common land in the drawing CL.
3. Mark the manor house M, mark the flour mill FM and mark the saw mill SM. Where did the mills get their power from?
5. Who were (a) landlords, (b) yeoman farmers, (c) husbandmen?
6. In many ways Tudor villages were 'self-sufficient'. What does this mean?
7. What effect would a bad harvest have on the life of a village ?
8. A typical village usually had several craftsmen including

   (a) a wheelwright,   (b) a carpenter,   (c) a blacksmith,
   (d) a weaver,   (e) a miller.

   What do you think these craftsmen did? Do these occupations exist today? If so, have they changed in any way?
9. During the Tudor period much of the common land began to disappear and was closed off (enclosed). Why did this happen? What was the enclosed land used for and why? How did this enclosure of common land affect the villagers? Mark the enclosed fields EF in the drawing.
10. Imagine you are a boy or girl living a Tudor village. Write a paragraph on a day in your life.

HOW THE TUDORS LIVED - A COTTAGE

Look at the drawing below which shows a typical Tudor cottage then answer the questions below it.

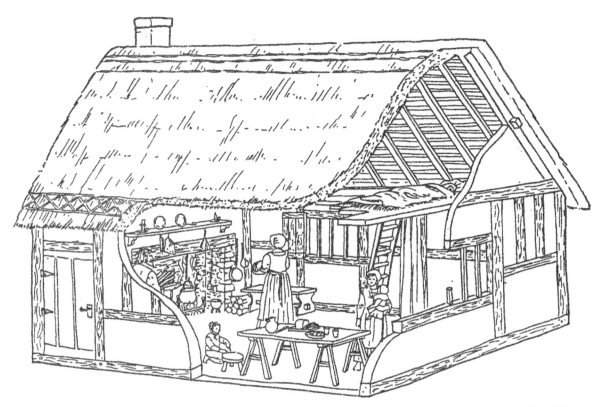

The cottage had one large room divided up and sometimes space in the loft. (This cottage was divided into a bedroom, a living room and a stable). Furniture and utensils included 1 table, 3 stools, 1 small bed, cooking utensils (2 pots, 3 porringers), 3 knives and 4 trenchers).

1. What were the walls of the cottage made of?

2. What was the roof made of?

3. Do you think the cottage would have had glass windows? If not what would have covered the window spaces?

4. How many 'rooms' were there and what were they used for?

5. How did the people reach the space upstairs?

6. Is the house well furnished?

7. Did all the family sit for meals?

8. What eating utensils did they have?

9. What was (a) a porringer, (b) a trencher?

10. What covered the floors of the cottage?

11. How do you think the cottage was (a) heated, (b) lit?

12. There is no bathroom in the cottage. How did the people wash?

13. Who would have lived in such a house?

14. Where would the family have kept an animal in the winter?

15. Compare this cottage with the place where you live.

HOW THE TUDORS LIVED
A MANOR HOUSE

Below is a drawing of a typical Tudor manor house. The accommodation included:
Ground Floor - hall, armoury, kitchen/pantry/buttery, parlour, a cubby hole, main entrance and porch.
Upper Floor - 3 bedrooms, 1 nursery, 1 house of office.
Below the Ground Floor - beer and wine cellars.
Adjoining the House - dairy, bakehouse and brewhouse.
The house furniture included: 3 feather beds, 3 linen chests, 1 cot, 6 tapestry wall coverings, 1 wooden table, 4 wooden chairs, 3 stools, 1 baby's stool, 2 wooden benches, 6 pewter candlesticks, 1 spinning wheel.

1. What were the frame and walls of this manor house made of?
2. What was the roof of the house made of?
3. Were there glass windows in this kind of house?
4. In which room did the family live?
5. What was the parlour used for?
6. What did the upstairs accommodation consist of?
7. What was a 'house of office' and what did it consist of in early Tudor houses?
8. Where was most of the cooking done?
9. What was a cubby hole and what was it used for?
10. A dairy, bakehouse and a brewhouse were next to the manor house. What does this suggest?
11. Why would such a house have a spinning wheel? Who would use it?
12. What was the armoury for?
13. Where would the water supply for the house have come from?
14. Who do you think would have lived in such a house?
15. Pretend you are living in the house in Tudor times. Discuss the benefits and problems of living there.

HOW THE TUDORS LIVED - A MANSION

Below is a drawing of a typical Tudor mansion. The accommodation included:
Main Rooms - large hall, dining room, long gallery, state apartments, numerous bedrooms, armoury, kitchens, library, chapel, solar, games room, closets, buttery, dairy, beer and wine cellars, servants' quarters.
Furniture - numerous rooms fitted with expensive furniture and wall coverings, family portraits, gold and silver plate.

1. What was this mansion made of?

2. Did this building have glass windows?

3. Was this mansion small, big, or very big?

4. What was a long gallery and what was it used for?

5. What was (a) a solar, (b) a buttery and (c) a closet?

6. What were 'family portraits'?

7. Who do you think lived in such a mansion?

8. What suggests the owner of this property was wealthy?

9. What does 'gold and silver plate' mean?

10. Imagine you own this mansion and Queen Elizabeth I is coming to stay.
Suggest what preparations you would have to make.

TUDOR TOWN LIFE

Look at the these drawings of town life in the Tudor period and today. Use them to answer the questions below.

1. Find ten differences between a Tudor town and a modern town.

2. Are there any similarities between the two?

3. What made life in a Tudor town difficult for the inhabitants?

4. What makes life pleasant in a modern town for the inhabitants?

5. Were there any advantages to living in Tudor times compared with life in a modern town today?

6. Give three dangers in a Tudor town and three dangers in a modern town to health and safety.

7. Write an imaginative account of a day in the life of one of these Tudors: a rich merchant, a housewife, a servant in a gentleman's house, a town beggar.

TUDOR LONDON

Below is a pictorial map of London in Tudor times. Look at this carefully and then answer the questions which follow it.

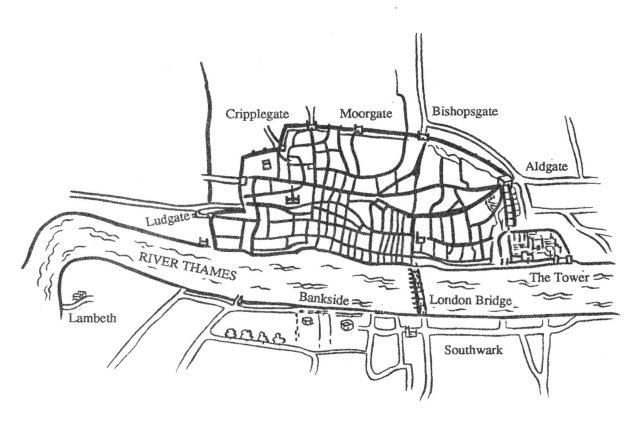

1. Through what gates in the medieval wall did people enter London?

2. What was the only bridge across the River Thames?

3. What does the map tell you about the numbers of people and houses in Lambeth and Southwark?

4. Why do you think people travelled along the Thames by barge instead of through the London streets?

5. From where did people in London get their water?

6. In 1500, London was the largest English city. How many people lived there? Was the city large by European standards?

7. What happened to the size of the population of London between 1560 and 1600.

8. What was the chief London residence of Tudor monarchs from 1530?

9. Why was Westminister Hall so important in Tudor times?

10. Westminster Abbey was one of the most important monasteries in early Tudor times. Explain why this was so. How had the situation changed by 1539?

11. What were London Livery Companies?

12. Why was the Royal Exchange building so important?

13. Who was John Stow? Give the title of the book he wrote on London.

14. Write a short description of London in Tudor times.

TUDOR EATING HABITS

This drawing shows a a wealthy family in Tudor times sitting down to eat a meal.

1. Why are the men wearing hats?
2. Did the children usually sit down at the table to eat?
3. Who would have served the food at this meal?
4. What did wealthy families drink at meal times? What did the poorer families drink?
5. What was an aquamanile used for?
6. How long did meals in wealthy households last? Choose from 15 minutes, 30 minutes, 1 hour, usually much longer than 1 hour.

You have to lay this table for a meal for two people in Tudor times.
Begin by drawing a white linen cloth on it.
Next cut out the utensils from the drawings below and place them on the table.
Draw a cross on any items that you would not use.

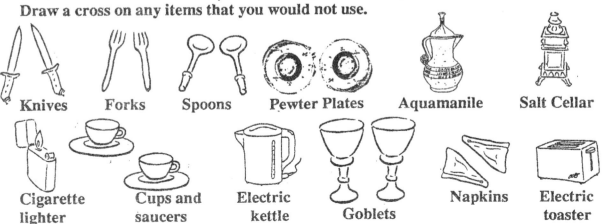

| Knives | Forks | Spoons | Pewter Plates | Aquamanile | Salt Cellar |

| Cigarette lighter | Cups and saucers | Electric kettle | Goblets | Napkins | Electric toaster |

A TUDOR DICTIONARY QUIZ

Fill in the boxes

MEANING	WORD
1. Follower of the House of York.	1.
2. Follower of the House of Lancaster.	2.
3. Dynasty which ruled from 1485 - 1603.	3.
4. Catholic Church Service.	4.
5. The New Learning.	5.
6. Radical religious change.	6.
7. The closing of the monasteries.	7.
8. Christian religion separate from Catholicism.	8.
9. Followers of Martin Luther.	9.
10. People who died for their beliefs.	10.
11. Those who paid fines in Elizabeth's day for not going to church.	11.
12. Concerned with the Pope.	12.
13. Barred from the Church by the Pope.	13.
14. Extreme Protestants.	14.
15. To obtain a legal separation from a wife or husband.	15.
16. Unbelievers.	16.
17. Catholic Court set up to examine and punish heretics.	17.
18. Disease spread by fleas on rats.	18.
19. Pen in Tudor times.	19.
20. A farm labourer in Tudor times.	20.

THE HOMELESS IN TUDOR TIMES

In the 16th century thousands of people were poor and without homes. Many wandered throughout the countryside looking for work or food and begging. This became so serious a problem that beggars, vagrants or vagabonds as they were called were whipped or mutilated: some were even put to death. Look at the print below and answer the questions that follow.

1. Is this print a primary or secondary source? Give a reason for your answer.

2. Give 3 other names for beggars in Tudor times.

3. In Tudor times poor people were described as the 'impotent' poor and the 'able-bodied'. Who were the impotent poor?

4. What was the Tudor attitude towards able-bodied beggars and vagabonds?

5. The print shows a beggar being whipped. Do you think he was one of the impotent or able-bodied poor?

6. Look at the other people in the print. Do you think they were sorry for for the beggar or glad that he was being punished?

7. Why do you think the beggar was being whipped?

8. Why do you think the beggar was tied to a rope with his hands bound behind him?

9. Where do you think the beggar was being led?

10. What was happening just outside the gate on the left hand side of the print?

11. Suggest two things that might happen to the beggar.

12. Comment on the beggar's dress and appearance.

13. Do we have beggars now? If so how do we treat them?

14. Suppose you were a beggar in Tudor times. Write an account of a day in your life.

CRIME AND PUNISHMENT

The print below shows Cuthbert Simson being tortured on the rack in the Tower of London in 1558. Answer the questions below it.

1. Is this a primary or secondary source? Give a reason for your answer.

2. What was the rack used for?

3. Who was Cuthbert Simnel?

4. Why was he being tortured and who had ordered this treatment?

5. Who are the men looking on?

6. What other forms of torture are shown in the print?

7. Write what you think the people in the print are saying in the bubbles below.

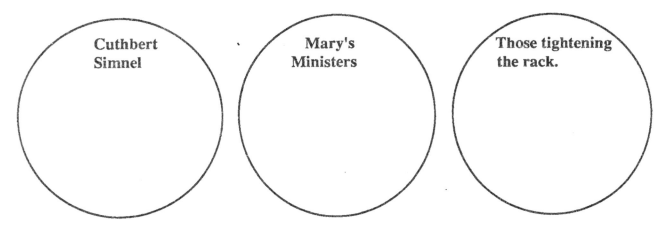

Cuthbert Simnel

Mary's Ministers

Those tightening the rack.

8. The Tudors were often very cruel. Give three examples of this cruelty not shown in the print.

TUDOR DRESS - MEN

Look at the drawing below which shows the typical clothes of a courtier in Tudor times. Label the following garments: doublet, wide puffed sleeves , a ruff, breeches, a cloak, silk stockings (hose), shoes, hat with feather.

1. This Tudor gentleman's head is bare. Was this usual in Tudor times?
2. How was the doublet attached to the breeches?
3. How do you know the diagram is of a nobleman after 1550?
4. How did these clothes differ from those of the ordinary working man?

Read the following passage which tells us about how Robert Dudley, the Earl of Leicester was dressed. Then answer the questions which follow it.

... apparelled all in white, his shoes of velvet, his socks of hose knit silk, his upper stocks of white velvet lined with cloth of silver, his doublet of silver, his jerkin white velvet drawn with silver, beautified with gold and precious stone, his girdle and scabbard white velvet, his robe white satin embroidered with gold a foot broad very curiously, his cap black velvet with a white feather, his collar of gold beset with precious stones, and his garter about his leg of St. George's order - a sight worthy the beholding.

The Black Book of Warwick.

5. Is this a primary or secondary source?
6. 'This passage summarises what gentlemen wore in Elizabeth's day.' True or false?
7. List the garments Leicester was wearing which are typical of Elizabethan times.
8. Do you think the Earl of Leicester was rich or poor? Give a reason for your opinion.
9. Give the meaning of the following:
    (a) embroidered with gold a foot broad,
    (b) his garter about his leg of St. George's order,
    (c) a sight worthy the beholding.
10. Draw and colour a picture of the Earl of Leicester.

TUDOR WOMEN

The drawings A and B show women at home in Tudor times.

1. What are the women in drawing A doing?
2. What are the women in drawing B doing?
3. One picture shows upper class women and the other shows lower class women. Which is which?
4. Which women worked the hardest in Tudor times?
5. How would the education of the women in A have differed from those in B?
6. Imagine you are a servant in an Elizabethan mansion. Your master and mistress are expecting important guests to stay with them for a while. Write an account of what you have to do in preparation for the visitors.

Look at the way in which the women in the drawings C and D are dressed.
7. Who is lower class and who is upper class?
8. Does the way in which the women are dressed depend on
   (a) their wealth and (b) the work they do? Give reasons for your answers.

THE RENAISSANCE
THE ARRIVAL OF THE PRINTING PRESS

Just before the reign of Henry VII printing by movable type was first used in Holland and Germany (about 1440). William Caxton visited Germany and brought a new press back to England in 1476. This invention meant that books which were previously written by hand by monks (called scribes) could now be printed. Separate letters made of metal were fixed in a metal frame and covered with a layer of ink. A page was pressed on the metal letters and an impression of the letters was made on the paper. When dry, the pages were bound into a book and by the end of the Tudor period thousands of books had been printed and were available to be read.

Look at this early engraving of a print shop and answer the questions below it.

1. How many printing presses can you see?
2. Why were these machines called 'printing presses'? What is being pressed?
3. In the print, find the screw for applying pressure in the press.
4. In the print, find the ink pot and the sponge or dabber for applying the ink.
5. What is the woman at the back of the print shop doing?
6. What is the young child in the front of the shop doing?
   What does this tell you about the use of child labour in the 16th century?
7. What is hanging on the lines between the presses? Why?
8. Make the initials of your name in Plasticine. Cover them with paint and press them on to a sheet of paper. Which way do the letters have to be placed on the paper? Would you be able to read the metal sheet of text easily before it was printed? Give a reason for your answer.
9. 'The arrival of the printing press using movable type was the most important event in the history of the Renaissance.' Do you agree? Give reasons for your answer.
10. Find out about modern printing presses.

THE BOKE OF HUSBANDRY, 1523
By Anthony Fitzherbert

This is the title page of an important book published in Tudor times. It was written for yeoman farmers and their wives.

1. Who was the author and when was the book published?

2. What is the word in large letters at the top of the picture? What does this word mean?

3. What are the two men in the picture doing?

Ḡ̄ere begynneth a newe tracte oȝ treatyſe mooſt pȝfytable foȝ all huſbāde men / and very frutefull foȝ all other perſones to rede / newly coȝrecte ɫ amended by the auctour / with dyuerſe other thynges added therunto.

Huſbondȝye

These are extracts from the book setting out the duties of a farmer's wife:

… first in a morning when thou art waked and proposeth to rise, take up thy hand and bless thee and make the sign of the holy cross. In nomine patris et filii et spiritus sancti Amen. In the name of the father, the son and the Holy Ghost. And if thou say a Pater Noster, an Ave and a Creed and remember thy Maker, thou shalt speed much the better.

… first sweep thy house, dress up they dishboard, and set all good things in order within thy house: milk thy kye, suckle thy calves, syc up thy milk, take up thy children and array them, and provide for thy husband's breakfast, dinner, supper and for thy children and servants, and take thy part with them. And to ordain corn and malt to the mill, to bake and brew withal when need is …

[boke - book, proposeth - getting ready, Pater Noster - a prayer, thy - your, kye - cow, syc up - strain, array - dress, ordain - send, withal - likewise]

4. Is this a primary or secondary source? Give a reason for your answer.
5. Make a list of the tasks a farmer's wife was expected to carry out according to these extracts.
6. Explain the words 'In nomine patris et filii et spiritus sancti.' In what language is this prayer written? How might it have changed after 1539?
7. Write a short account of the life of a farmer's wife in Tudor times.
8. How does this compare with the life of a farmer's wife today?

MEDICINE IN TUDOR TIMES

In 1538 the citizens of London petitioned Henry VIII to re-found hospitals closed in the dissolution of 1536 (when monasteries, nunneries and chantries were also closed). Answer the questions which follow this petition.

We petition the Sovereign ...

... For the aid and comfort of the poor sick, blind, aged and impotent persons, being not able to help themselves, nor having any place certain wherein they may be lodged, cherished and refreshed till they be cured and holpen of their disease and sickness. For the help of the said poor people, we inform your Grace that there be near or within the City of London three hospitals or spitels, commonly called Saint Mary Spitel, Saint Bartholomew Spitel, and Saint Thomas Spitel, founded of good devotion by ancient fathers and endowed with great possessions and rents ...

They wanted to refound the hospitals for very sound reasons.

... a great number of poor, needy, sick and indigent persons shall be refreshed, maintained, comforted, found, healed and cured of their infirmities, frankly and freely by physicians, surgeons and apothecaries ... so that all impotent persons not able to labour shall be relieved and all sturdy beggars not willing to labour shall be punished, so that with God's grace few or no persons shall be seen abroad to beg or ask alms.

1. What was a 'spital' or 'spitel'? Name three spitels in London mentioned in the petition.

2. What were 'impotent' persons? In what way were they regarded as different from other homeless poor in Tudor times?

3. What were physicians, surgeons and apothecaries?

4. Why did people want the hospitals restored? (Include the economic reasons.)

5. Much of Tudor medicine depended on the twin remedies of diet and bloodletting. What do you know about these treatments?

6. What were 'cupping' glasses and leeches?
   Explain how they were used in Tudor times.

7. (a) What were the main serious diseases that occurred in Tudor times?
   (b) How did the living conditions of the time contribute to the spread of such diseases?
   (c) Do these diseases occur today?

8. Imagine you are a Tudor doctor. What advice would you give to a young person suffering from a fever and a headache.

9. This table is a summary of Tudor theories on medicine. Fill in the blank spaces.

BLOOD	SANGUINE
....	PHLEGMATIC
WHITE BILE	....
BLACK BILE	MELANCHOLIC
EARTH	....
AIR	HOT
....	MOIST
WATER	DRY

SPORTS AND PASTIMES

Look at the woodcut below taken from Holinshed's 'Chronicles of England', 1577, then answer the questions which follow it.

A

1. Print A shows a joust. What was a joust?
2. Who took part in jousts?
3. Was this a pastime for wealthy or poor people?
4. Describe what is happening in the print.
5. The contestants included Henry VIII incognito. What does 'incognito' mean?
6. What is the long pole carried by the rider on the left called? What has happened to his opponent's?
7. What do you think the man waving his arm in the middle of the picture is doing?
8. There is another combatant at the back right hand side of the picture. What is he doing?
9. Do you think such contests were dangerous? Give any fact you know to illustrate the dangers or potential dangers.
10. How would the spectators recognise the combatants when they were wearing armour?

B

C

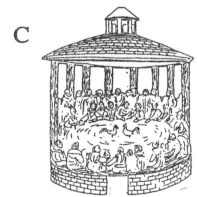

13. What is the name of the building in drawing C? What happened in C?
14. The pastime in C is regarded as a cruel sport. What other Tudor pastimes were cruel?

11. What game is being played in print B?
12. How does this Tudor game differ from the modern game?

15. What do you know about 'foteball' in Tudor times? How did it differ from the game of football played in this country today?

THE TUDOR NAVY

A Typical Tudor Ship

1. Label these parts of the ship in the drawing above: foremast, mainmast, mizzenmast, bowsprit, forecastle, gunport.

2. Imagine you are a sailor on a Tudor ship. Write an account of a day in your life.

3. 'The life of an officer in the Tudor navy was better than that of a sailor.' In what ways was this true?

4. 'Discipline was strict and punishment was harsh.' Do you think such treatment was necessary? Outline the main ways in which sailors were punished.

5. Explain why it was impossible to provide fresh food and water for the crew on long journeys. What were the effects of this?

6. Explain the meaning of the nautical terms
   (a) portside, (b) starboard, (c) keelhauling, (d) broadside.

7. When Henry VIII came to the throne, there were just 5 ships in the navy. When he died there were 56. Give a brief account of the way in which the King built up the navy. He set up the 'King's Majesty Council of the Marine'. What did this become?

8. Why did Henry VIII build up the navy?

9. What major engagement with an enemy showed the strength of the English navy in Elizabeth's day? Name three famous naval commanders at this time.

THE 'MARY ROSE'

The 'Mary Rose' was built in Portsmouth on the orders of Henry VIII. When the King reviewed the fleet in March 1513, she was described as the best and fastest vessel afloat. Tragically, in July 1545 during a battle against the French (the Battle of the Solent), she capsized and was lost together with many of her crew.

1. A French account of the sinking of the ship suggested she was destroyed by cannon from French ships. Francis van der Delft, Ambassador to Charles V relates the following account.

   … I made enquiries of one of the survivors as to why the ship sank. He told me that the disaster was caused by their not having closed the lowest row of gun ports on one side of the ship. Having fired the guns on that side, the ship was turning, in order to fire from the other, when the wind caught her sails so strongly as to heel her over, and plunge her open gun-ports beneath the water which flooded and sank her …

   Which do you think is the most likely cause? Give reasons for your answer.

2. Imagine you are a reporter. Write an account of the sinking of the 'Mary Rose'. Begin 'I am watching …'

3. 'The *Mary Rose* is a time capsule of Tudor life.' What does this mean and why is it important?

4. Outline five things about Tudor life at sea that can be discovered from a study of the 'Mary Rose.'

5. The 'Mary Rose' was a fighting ship. How was the ship specially designed for this role?

6. Fighting ships were used for soldiers to board enemy ships. How did the design of ships like the 'Mary Rose' change the way in which sea battles were fought?

THE SPANISH ARMADA, 1588

This drawing shows the initial battle off the Isle of Wight.

1. Who launched the Armada? Give five reasons why it was sent.
2. Why did the Armada sail in 1588 and not earlier?
3. Name (a) the Spanish commander and (b) two English leaders in this sea battle.
4. What were the Spanish ships trying to do?
5. How did the English ships make the Spanish vessels keep their distance?
6. Pretend you are a reporter present at the battle. Write an account of it. Begin 'I am at the battle between our brave ships and the Spanish Armada ...'
7. The Spanish ships retreated to a French port. Name the port.
   The English sent fire-ships into the Spanish vessels at anchor. What does this mean?
8. Describe what happened to the Spanish Armada after this first defeat by the English. How many of their ships eventually returned to Spain?

9. This map shows part of the route of the Spanish Armada. Mark the following on the map.
   (a) South West England.   (b) The Lizard   (c) The Isle of Wight
   (d) The French coast   (e) Calais   (f) To Scotland
10. Imagine you are Sir Francis Drake. Write a letter to Queen Elizabeth describing your success over the Spanish Armada.
11. How did Queen Elizabeth react (a) to Philip II sending the Armada; (b) to its defeat?

EXPLORATION IN TUDOR TIMES

[Use World Map at the end of the Worksheets.]

1. Many voyages of discovery were made in the 15th and 16th centuries including:

    1486 Bartholomew Diaz sailed around the southern tip of Africa.

    1492 Christopher Columbus reached the Indies (the West Indies).

    1497 John Cabot discovered Newfoundland.

    1498 Vasco da Gama discovered India.

    1521 Ferdinand Magellan reached the Philippines.

    Mark the routes of these explorers on the map.

2. Find out the routes and discoveries of Amerigo Vespucci, Hernando Cortes, Francisco Pizarro and Sir Francis Drake.

3. (a) Why were explorations undertaken at this time?
   (b) What did England gain from them?

4. What dangers did these explorers face
   (a) at sea?
   (b) when they arrived and discovered 'new' lands?

5. (a) How did these explorers navigate?
   (b) What aids to navigation do we have today that were not available to these explorers?

6. These voyages cast doubt on the traditional belief about the shape of the world. Explain.

7. Draw a sketch map to trace a journey you have made in one of the following circumstances:
   (a) the journey from your home to your school.
   (b) the journey from your home to a relative or friend living nearby.
   (c) the journey from your home to a relative or friend living some distance away.
   Include any landmarks on your map.

8. Use maps to trace the journey you have made in one or both of the following:
   (a) a holiday in the UK.
   (b) a holiday abroad.
   How did you travel (on foot, by car, by plane, by boat ...)?

9. What 'voyages of discovery' are being made today?

10. Where do you think future explorers will travel? How will they travel?

FAMOUS TUDORS

The following are drawings of some famous Tudors followed by a list of their actions, achievements, records, inventions, writings or works of art. Write the correct caption under each drawing. The first one has been done for you.

THOMAS CRANMER

Archbishop of Canterbury

BESS OF HARDWICK

WILLIAM SHAKESPEARE
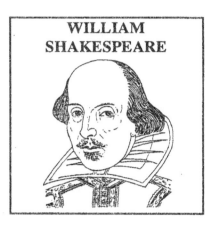

LADY JANE GREY

WILLIAM CECIL

RICHARD BURBAGE

THOMAS WOLSEY

SIR FRANCIS DRAKE

DESIDERIUS ERASMUS
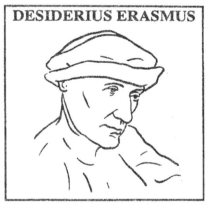

HENRY VII
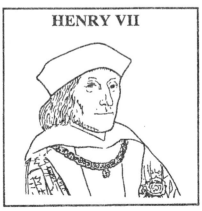

CAPTIONS
Founder of Tudor Dynasty
The Nine Days' Queen
Dutch Scholar
Countess of Shrewsbury
Playwright who built the Globe
Archbishop of Canterbury
Elizabethan Statesman
Helped to defeat the Armada
Elizabethan actor
Built Hampton Court

TUDOR QUIZ

Try these questions

1. Who founded the Tudor dynasty?

2. Who was defeated at Bosworth Field?

3. Give the dates of the start and end of the Tudor dynasty.

4. Who was defeated at Flodden Field and when?

5. Who was Cardinal Wolsey?

6. Who did Henry VIII meet at the Field of the Cloth of Gold?

7. What title did the Pope give Henry VIII for defending the Roman Catholic faith against Luther? Does the monarch still have this title today?

8. Who did Henry VIII want to marry when he wanted to divorce Catherine of Aragon? What was the main reason for him wanting this separation?

9. Did Anne Boleyn give Henry VIII a male heir? Who was her child?

10. Name Henry VIII's famous warship which sank in the Solent.

11. Who was nicknamed the 'Mare of Flanders' and why?

12. Name the famous German painter who painted portraits of the Tudor monarchs.

13. When did the Reformation Parliament first meet?

14. Name the Protectors in Edward VI's reign.

15. Name the Nine Days' Queen.

16. Who was Bloody Mary and why was she so called? Give the dates of her reign.

17. When did Elizabeth I come to the throne?

18. Which country was England's worse enemy
    (a) at the beginning of the Tudor period?
    (b) at the end of the Tudor period?

19. Who was Rizzio?

20. Who or what was Babington's Plot?

21. Name the Scottish Queen related to Queen Elizabeth who was executed in 1587. Who signed her death warrant?

22. Who was the King of Spain in the reign of Elizabeth I?

23. Name the Spanish fleet that sailed against Elizabeth in 1588.

24. Who was the Duke of Medina Sidonia?

25. What do you understand by the word 'Renaissance'?

26. What important invention was brought to England by William Caxton?

27. The invention in 26 led to many - - - - - for people to read.

28. Who or what was Desiderius Erasmus?

29. What was a recusant in Elizabeth I's time?

30. What was the plague?

TUDOR OBJECTS

Put a X through the items below which were NOT available in Tudor times.

Pewter plates

Quill

Arquebus

Printing press

Calculator

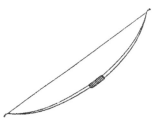

Computer

Aquamanile

Can of Coke

Longbow

Telephone

Leather Shoe

Fountain pen

Crossbow

Lute

Candle

Comb

Canon

Backgammon Board

Crisps

WILLIAM SHAKESPEARE

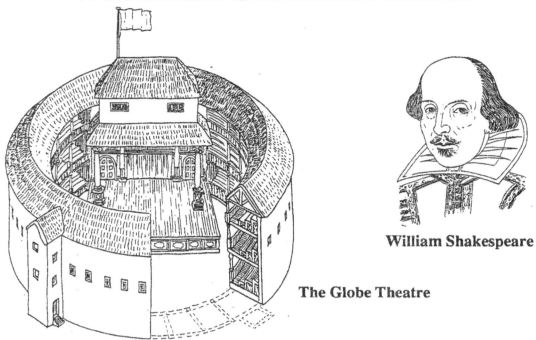

William Shakespeare

The Globe Theatre

1. Who was William Shakespeare and where was he born?

2. Name any 3 plays that Shakespeare wrote.

3. Where was the Globe Theatre situated?

4. A new theatre has been built in London exactly where Shakespeare's theatre was in the 16th century. Describe the Globe using the drawing above (and if possible visit the 'new' Globe Theatre).
   [What kind of stage did it have? Did it have a roof? Were refreshments available? How did the audience behave in Shakespeare's time?]

5. Imagine you are going to the Globe to see a play Shakespeare has just written. Describe your visit.

6. How does Shakespeare's Globe differ from an ordinary theatre today?

7. Where did travelling actors perform in Tudor times? Is there any similar tradition today?

8. Shakespeare's plays were accompanied by music. Name the Tudor instruments drawn below. Choose from:
   viol, lute, virginal, shawm, recorder, trumpet, clavichord, harp, tabor, flute.

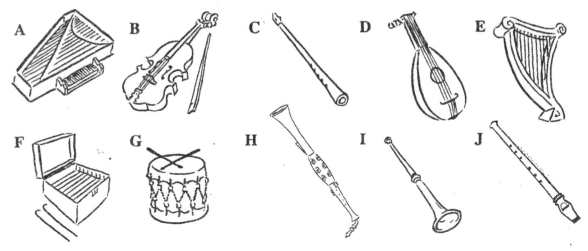

THE TUDOR LEGACY

Make this Tudor Legacy Wheel the centre of a Tudor Legacy Wall.
Below are some suggestions for your Wall.

1. England as a world power. Pinpoint the defeat of the Armada.

2. England as the centre of Protestanism with France and Spain leaders of Roman Catholic Europe.

3. Navy - beginning of naval power. Include naval shipyards and the beginning of the admiralty.

4. Trade - Rise of London trading companies. Beginning of East India Company.

5. Discovery of new lands. Drake's world voyage. Pinpoint lands discovered.

6. Other discoveries: tobacco and potatoes by Sir Walter Raleigh; mathematical symbols (+, -, = signs were first used in Tudor times); chimneys first used in Tudor times; in 1570 a Spaniard invented the first toothbrush; astronomers argued that the earth moved around the sun; the earth was shown to be round and not flat. Also - the screw, the pencil, the first pocket watch. Very important - the PRINTING PRESS and PRINTING.

7. Architecture and building - make a note of famous houses and mansions. Brickworks established and also glassworks in England. Brick buildings constructed.

8. Tudor Renaissance - Shakespeare, Ben Jonson, Christopher Marlowe. Buildings of theatres and the music of Byrd.

TUDOR DOCUMENTS
DESIGN YOUR OWN
A LETTER FROM QUEEN ELIZABETH I

Dab a piece of white paper all over with a wet tea bag. (Do not stain your clothes.) Lie it flat and leave in a cool place to dry completely. Next cut a wavy pattern along the edges of the paper.

The letter below written by Queen Elizabeth I was given to Mary, Queen of Scots, at the opening of her trial at Fotheringay Castle on 12 October, 1586.

October 1586

You have in various ways and manners attempted to take my life and to bring my kingdom to destruction by bloodshed. I have never proceeded so harshly against you, but have, on the contrary, protected and maintained you like myself. These treasons will be proved to you and all made manifest. Yet it is my will, that you answer the nobles and peers of the kingdom as if I were myself present. I therefore require, charge, and command that you make answer for I have been well informed of your arrogance.

Act plainly without reserve, and you will sooner be able to obtain favour of me.

Elisabeth R

Write this letter on the paper you have prepared then fold it and close it with the Queen's seal. [See the bottom of this page.] Use the blank beside this seal to design other seals - e.g. use Plasticine on red ribbon.

SEALS

In Tudor times there were no envelopes like we have today. Letters were folded several times, and closed with a seal so that they could not be opened. They were then sent by messenger. A seal was a piece of stone or metal (often a signet ring) with the private mark of the writer engraved on it. This mark could be a coat of arms but in the case of royalty it bore a picture of the sender. The mark was pressed into soft sealing wax which closed the document. Some seals also had a signature or a few words written on them. These words were known as the legend and usually gave the name and rank of the owner.

Other suggestions for Tudor documents:
(a) A bill of sale from one merchant to another.
(b) A peace treaty made between two countries.
Design seals for the documents. Explain why a Tudor Rose made out of pink and white Plasticine would be suitable.

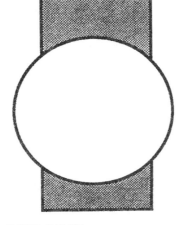

The Tudor Rose

TUDOR TIME-LINE

Select the correct date for each of the events below. Choose from:

1485, 1497, 1502, 1509, 1512, 1520, 1533, 1536-9, 1547, 1554, 1558, 1586, 1587, 1588, 1597, 1603.

DATE   EVENT

_____ Death of Arthur, Prince of Wales. _____

_____ Henry VIII marries Anne Boleyn. _____

_____ New Poor Law Legislation gives relief to the impotent poor.
(Renacted 1601.) _____

_____ Death of Henry VIII. _____

_____ Accession of Elizabeth I. _____

_____ John Cabot sails to Newfoundland. _____

_____ Death of Elizabeth I. _____

_____ Accession of Henry VIII.
Marriage with Catherine of Aragon. _____

_____ Defeat of the Spanish Armada. _____

_____ Dissolution of the monasteries. _____

_____ Babington Plot.
Trial of Mary Queen of Scots. _____

_____ Accession of Henry VII. _____

_____ Wolsey becomes Henry VIII's Chief Minister. _____

_____ Henry VIII meets Francis I of France at the Field of the
Cloth of Gold. _____

_____ Mary Tudor marries Philip II of Spain. _____

_____ Execution of Mary Queen of Scots. _____

Now write these events and dates in the correct chronological order to make a Tudor time-line. Add any other events and their dates that you think are important.

TUDOR WORDSEARCH

Below the square are the clues to the words hidden in the square. The words may be forwards, backwards, upside down or diagonal and any letter may be used once, more than once or not at all.

```
A  N  N  E  C  I  T  E  R  E  H  A  T  S
S  B  T  O  L  P  L  A  G  U  E  E  R  T
R  O  S  E  M  A  R  Y  T  A  I  L  O  R
E  L  L  T  A  O  M  O  N  A  R  C  H  I
N  E  L  I  Z  A  B  E  T  H  E  P  O  P
A  Y  I  R  O  N  A  M  O  E  S  U  R  S
I  N  U  Y  E  S  L  O  W  T  C  S  N  F
S  T  Q  U  E  E  N  O  E  D  S  T  B  F
S  A  G  N  I  T  N  I  R  P  R  U  O  U
A  D  M  I  R  A  L  T  Y  J  R  A  O  R
N  A  F  R  A  N  C  I  S  S  E  E  K  J
C  M  M  O  N  A  S  T  E  R  I  E  S  E
E  R  E  F  O  R  M  A  T  I  O  N  E  S
W  A  L  L  G  L  O  B  E  C  R  O  W  N
```

1. Ruled instead of Edward VI.
2. Spread by fleas on rats.
3. Mother of Elizabeth I.
4. Sovereign.
5. Successor to the sovereign.
6. Spanish fleet.
7. Led English fleet against 6.
8. Henry VIII's ship which sank in 1545.
9. Shakespeare's theatre.
10. House of middle class Tudor gentleman.
11. Thomas who built Hampton Court.
12. Land for cultivation was divided into these.
13. Tudor symbol.
14. Someone who dies for his/her beliefs.
15. Tudor collar.
16. Worn at coronation.
17. Pens from feathers.
18. Tudor single page educational aid.
19. Made books available generally.
20. Rebirth.
21. Religious organisations closed by Henry VIII.
22. Combat between knights.
23. Developed from the King's Majesty Council of the Marine.
24. Surrounded London.
25. London castle used for prisoners.
26. Last Tudor monarch.
27. Religous movement in the 16th century.
28. Plan to dethrone the sovereign.
29. Head of Roman Catholic Church.
30. Justice of the Peace.
31. A bishop's diocese.
32. Water surrounding a castle.
33. Makes clothes and garments.
34. Person in 33 does this with a needle and thread.
35. Worn by Tudor men even at meals.
36. Cut down for wood for ships and houses.
37. French were defeated at Guinegate in 1513 and Henry VIII - - - his spurs.
38. Trick or ploy.
39. Ridges in roads.

How many words can you make from the letters in
THE TUDOR DYNASTY?
(25 - fair, 50 - good, 75 - very good, 100 - excellent, over 100 - genius.)

A TUDOR RECIPE
APPLE MOUSSE

Try this Tudor recipe.
[Ask an adult before using the cooker.]

Take a dozen apples and ether rooste or boyle them and drawe them thorowe a streyner, and the yolkes of three or foure egges withal, and, as ye strayne them, temper them wyth three or foure sponefull of damaske water yf ye wyll, than take and season it wyth suger and halfe a dysche of swete butter, and boyle them upon a chaffyngdysche in a platter, and caste byskettes or synamon and gynger upon them and so serve them forth.

What do you think these words mean in the recipe?

ether, rooste or boyle, streyner, temper them, damaske water, suger, swete butter, synamon, gynger, serve them forth.

A MODERN VERSION

Ingredients
METRIC

Ingredients
IMPERIAL

METRIC	IMPERIAL
700 g apples	$1\frac{1}{2}$ lb apples
45 ml water	3 tbls water
2 egg yolks	2 egg yolks
30 ml rosewater	2 tbls rosewater
30 ml sugar	2 tbls sugar
25 g butter	1 oz butter
pinch ground ginger and cinnamon	pinch ground ginger and cinnamon

Peel, core and slice the apples.

Gently heat the apples in the water in a saucepan until they are soft.

Purée the apples using a blender or sieve.

Place the purée back in the saucepan.

Beat the egg yolks with the rosewater and add to the purée.

Then stir in the sugar and butter.

Slowly heat the apple mixture until it just boils, stirring continuously.

Pour into a dish and allow to cool before serving.

Sprinkle with a little ground ginger and cinnamon.

(Delicious with ice cream.)

A TUDOR GAME

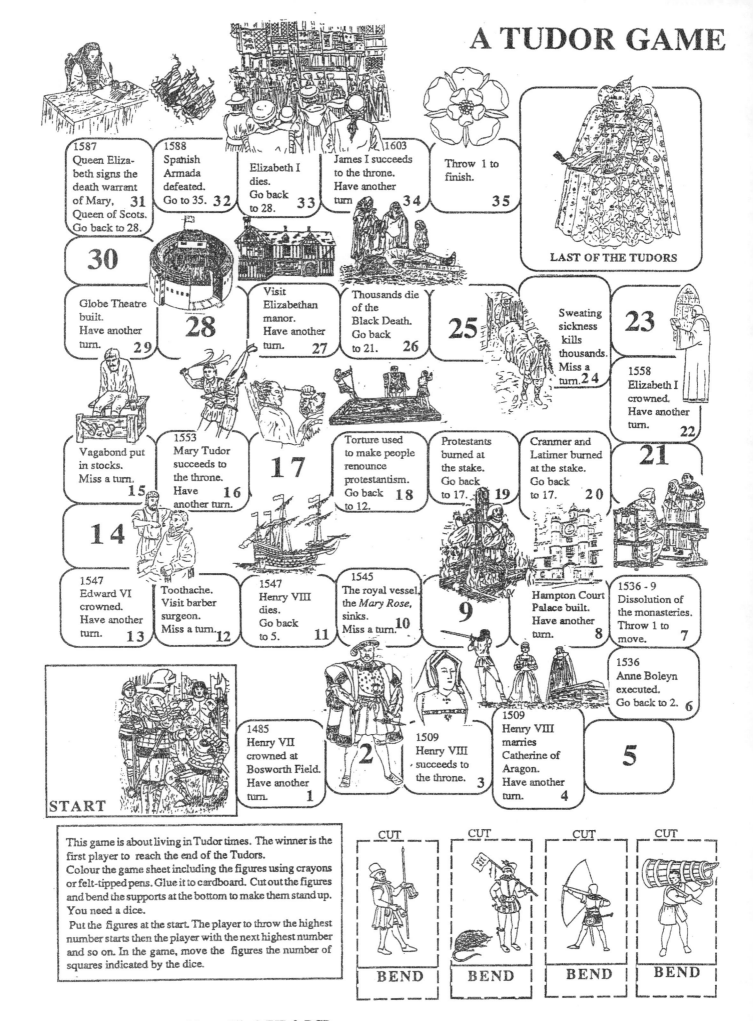

1587 Queen Elizabeth signs the death warrant of Mary, Queen of Scots. Go back to 28. **31**

1588 Spanish Armada defeated. Go to 35. **32**

1603 Elizabeth I dies. Go back to 28. **33**

James I succeeds to the throne. Have another turn. **34**

Throw 1 to finish. **35**

LAST OF THE TUDORS

30

28

Globe Theatre built. Have another turn. **29**

Visit Elizabethan manor. Have another turn. **27**

Thousands die of the Black Death. Go back to 21. **26**

25

Sweating sickness kills thousands. Miss a turn. **24**

23

1558 Elizabeth I crowned. Have another turn. **22**

Vagabond put in stocks. Miss a turn. **15**

1553 Mary Tudor succeeds to the throne. Have another turn. **16**

17

Torture used to make people renounce protestantism. Go back to 12. **18**

Protestants burned at the stake. Go back to 17. **19**

Cranmer and Latimer burned at the stake. Go back to 17. **20**

21

14

1547 Edward VI crowned. Have another turn. **13**

Toothache. Visit barber surgeon. Miss a turn. **12**

1547 Henry VIII dies. Go back to 5. **11**

1545 The royal vessel, the *Mary Rose*, sinks. Miss a turn. **10**

9

Hampton Court Palace built. Have another turn. **8**

1536 - 9 Dissolution of the monasteries. Throw 1 to move. **7**

1536 Anne Boleyn executed. Go back to 2. **6**

START

1485 Henry VII crowned at Bosworth Field. Have another turn. **1**

2

1509 Henry VIII succeeds to the throne. **3**

1509 Henry VIII marries Catherine of Aragon. Have another turn. **4**

5

This game is about living in Tudor times. The winner is the first player to reach the end of the Tudors.
Colour the game sheet including the figures using crayons or felt-tipped pens. Glue it to cardboard. Cut out the figures and bend the supports at the bottom to make them stand up. You need a dice.
Put the figures at the start. The player to throw the highest number starts then the player with the next highest number and so on. In the game, move the figures the number of squares indicated by the dice.

CUT — BEND
CUT — BEND
CUT — BEND
CUT — BEND

Life in Tudor Times Master File © EJP & DCP

PROJECT IDEAS

1. Life in Tudor Times.
2. Tudor Kings and Queens.
3. Food and Diet in Tudor Times.
4. Tudor Clothes - Men.
5. Tudor Clothes - Women.
6. Women in Tudor Times.
7. Yeoman Farmers.
8. Tudor Gentlemen.
9. Nobles and Nobility in Tudor Times.
10. The Tudor Navy.
11. The Reformation.
12. The Renaissance.
13. Famous Tudor Poets.
14. Famous Tudor Discoveries.
15. Voyages of Discovery.
16. Famous Tudors.
17. Apprentices in Tudor Times.
18. Tudor Homes - Mansions.
19. Tudor Palaces.
20. Thomas Wolsey.
21. Sir William Cecil.
22. Sir Thomas Gresham.
23. Roads and Travel in Tudor Times.
24. Vagabonds and Rogues in Tudor Times.
25. Furniture and Furnishings in Tudor Times.
26. Portrait Painters and Paintings.
27. Tudor Merchants.
28. A Visit to a Tudor House.
29. Local Government in Tudor Times.
30. Famous Tudor Women.
31. Printing and Books in Tudor Times.
32. Tudor Towns.
33. Tudor London.
34. Tudor Musical Instruments.
35. Tudor Music.
36. Medicine in Tudor Times.
37. Famous Tudor Doctors.
38. Trade and Commerce in Tudor Times.
39. Tudor Defences.
40. Tudor Coins and Coinage.
41. Tudor Inns and Hostelries.
42. Elizabethan English.
43. Crime and Punishment.
44. Sports in Tudor Times.
45. Tudor Pastimes.
46. Tudor Documents.
47. Tudor Prints.
48. Court Life in Tudor Times.
49. Tudor Village Life.
50. Tudor Weapons.

THINGS TO MAKE

1. Model of a Tudor ship.
2. A Tudor bookmark.
3. A Tudor brooch.
4. A Tudor paperweight.
   (Paint a Tudor sailor on a smooth pebble or shell.)
5. A Tudor sword.
6. A Tudor helmet.
7. A Tudor hat.
8. A desk tidy decorated with Tudor drawings.
9. A tidy box decorated with Tudor drawings.
10. A Tudor needlework sampler.
11. A hornbook.
12. Make a Tudor cottage.
13. Make a feather pen.
14. Puppets of Tudor characters for a Tudor play.
15. A joker or jester.
16. A Tudor name plate.
17. A Tudor coin.
18. A Tudor banner.
19. A mask for a Tudor masque or party.
20. A Tudor rose.

WORLD MAP

Use this map with the worksheet Exploration in Tudor Times.

ANSWERS

Of course, there may be several alternative,
or additional acceptable answers to some of the questions.

Page 56

1. Five (Six if you include Lady Jane Grey). See Teachers' Notes.
2. No. Dates of the reigns. 3. 1547.
4. (a) Mary Tudor- 5 years.
   (b) Elizabeth I - 45 years.
5. (a) Henry VIII - 6 wives.
   (b) Edward VI; Elizabeth I.
   (c) Henry VII - 4 children.
6. (a) Mary Tudor - Catherine of Aragon, (b) Edward VI - Jane Seymour, (c) Elizabeth I - Anne Boleyn.
7. Lady Jane Grey.
8. True. Arthur, his elder brother, had died and he married Arthur's widow, Catherine of Aragon.
9. Margaret.
10. It united the Houses of Lancaster and York.

Page 57

See Teachers' Notes.

Page 58

1. Passage A - primary source. It was written in Tudor times.
2. Passage B - secondary source. Something written about an historical event or person some time later.
3. Any from *excelleth, divers, six score, thinketh, crosseth*.
4. The sweating sickness or the sweat. Influenza.
5. 1517, 1528, 1551.
6. Came on quickly and characterised by sweating profusely, very thirsty.
7. Men.
8. They were afraid of it and avoided contact with those who had the disease.
9. Anne Boleyn. She got over it quickly.
10. Gave the patient nothing to drink, kept the person in bed covered with blankets with arms crossed to avoid air reaching the patient's armpits.
11. Cholera or the plague.
12. They had little scientific or medical knowledge and depended on medieval remedies.

Page 59

1. No. The children were educated by different teachers all in one room.
2. Yes. There is a music chart on the wall at the back of room.
3. Yes. Some of the children are holding up books and there is a pile of books behind the teacher in the front on the right of the print.
4. Yes. There are several charts on the walls.
5. Yes. In the middle of the print to the front there is a boy playing with another boy's head.
6. Very severely. On the left of the print, a boy is held down while he is flogged by a master.
7. Reading is taught using the hornbooks on the left of the print; someone is writing at the back of the print on the right. The teacher at the front seems to be counting and teaching arithmetic.
8. Both.
9. Yes, one is visible in the print.
10. A quill - a pen. The man at the back of the picture on the right is using one.

11. No. The first pencils were made in 1565 in Switzerland. They were very expensive in Tudor times and were <u>not</u> generally available.
12. Ink- soot mixed with water.
13. Hornbook - a sheet of paper with writing on it mounted on a wooden board and protected by a sheet of transparent horn. They were also called criss-cross books because the first line started with a cross. They were used because all books were handwritten and only a few were available. They became less important later in Tudor times because of the invention of the printing press.
14. See Teachers' Notes.

Page 60

Catherine of Aragon - divorced, Anne Boleyn - beheaded, Jane Seymour - died - Anne, of Cleves - divorced, Catherine Howard - beheaded, Catherine Parr - outlived him.

1. Original (primary) source.
2 - 3. See Teachers' Notes.

Page 61

3. All of them.
4 - 5. See Teachers' Notes.

Page 62

1. See Teachers' Notes.
2. Primary. It was written by Edward VI.
3. Edward VI.
4. Elizabeth. Queen Elizabeth I.
5. Henry VIII and Jane Seymour. She died.
6. The Duke of Norfolk and Suffolk and the Archbishop of Canterbury.
7. Certain women.
8. Dr Cox, John Cheke and John Belmaine. Languages, philosophy, liberal sciences and French.
9. *Learning of tongues* - languages, *yere of our L* - year of our Lord.
10. 1547.
11. Final form at teachers' discretion.

Page 63

1. Heresy - not believing in the true religion. Martyr - a person who dies for his/her religious beliefs.
2. To make them repent for not following the true faith. Their souls were saved.
3. See Teachers' Notes.

Page 64

1. 1553. 16 years old.
2. (a) Cousin, (b) Daughter-in-law.
3. See Teachers' Notes.
4. Lady Jane Grey to succeed him and not his Catholic sister, Mary.
5. No. Conspirators and Lady Jane Grey were executed for treason. Mary Tudor.
6. A, D, C, B.

Page 65

1. Primary.
2. (c), (d) and (e).
3. *Discontent* - dissatisfaction/displeasure, *mute* - silent, *inwardly* - inside myself, *prate* - speak/chatter.

4. Elizabeth thought he was overbearing and deceitful. *Brainsick* - mad, *ruin* - downfall, *unkingly* - not worthy of a king, *treating peace* - making friendly overtures, *wrongful* - unjust.
5. Yes. The Spanish Armada failed.
6. She was courageous.
7. Philip II.
8. Elizabeth wanted Essex to carry out her orders. He did not follow instructions and was indecisive. She argues that he did not really want to succeed. He was eventually imprisoned in the Tower and executed.
9. See Teachers' Notes.
10. Regina - Queen.

Page 66
1. Linlithgow Castle, Scotland, on 8 December, 1542.
2. 1543. She was nine months old.
3. Dauphin Francis of France. 2 years.
4. James V of Scotland and Mary, Queen of Scots.
5. She had a good claim through her grandfather, Henry VII.
6. See Teachers' Notes.
7. The Northern Earls', Throgmorton's, Ridolfi's and Babington's plots.
8. Elizabeth I. 1587.
9. Fotheringay Castle, Northamptonshire, 1587.

Page 67
See Teachers' Notes.

Page 68
1. Rat catcher, 2. archer, 3. tinder box man, 4. chimney sweep, 5. printer, 6. jester, 7. candle maker, 8. water carrier, 9. town crier (bellman), 10. bear minder.

Page 69
See Teachers' Notes.

Page 70
See Teachers' Notes.

Page 71
See Teachers' Notes.

Page 72.
See Teachers' Notes.

Page 73
See Teachers' Notes.

Page 74
See Teachers' Notes.

Page 75
See Teachers' Notes.

Page 76
1. Yorkist 2. Lancastrian 3. Tudor 4. Mass
5. Renaissance 6. Reformation 7. Dissolution
8. Protestantism 9. Lutheran 10. Martyrs 11. Recusants
12. Papal 13. Excommunicated 14. Puritans 15. Divorce
16. Heretics 17. Inquisition 18. Plague 19. Quill
20. Husbandman.

Page 77
1. Primary. It was printed in the 16th century.
2. Choose from: Vagrants, vagabonds, rogues, poor, impotent poor, able-bodied poor.

3. People unable to earn their living because they were old, infirm or sick.
4. That they were lazy, did not want to work and should be severely punished.
5. Probably able-bodied.
6. Glad.
7. To discourage him from staying, to make him want to leave and to punish him for begging.
8. So that he could not escape until he was out of the town.
9. Out of the town so that he would not be a burden on the people. [They had to support the poor with money.]
10. Someone was being hanged.
11. He might be hanged or mutilated.
12. He was naked to the waist, he did not seem to have washed or shaved. He had long hair and a beard. He was unkempt.

Page 78
1. Primary. It is a contemporary woodcut.
2. To torture a prisoner. It 'stretched' the prisoner exerting a great deal of pain to make him confess to crimes or heresy and to make him reveal the names of others who might have been involved.
3. A Protestant sympathiser.
4. He was suspected of heresy and the torture was intended to make him confess. Queen Mary's courts.
5. Mary Tudor's Ministers.
6. Putting an arrow through a prisoner's fingers (left), the Scavenger's Daughter' (right), a device which squeezed the prisoner tighter and tighter.
7. Cuthbert Simnel: I have nothing to say.
   Mary's Ministers: Confess and we can stop the torture.
   Those tightening the rack: Shall we turn it another rachet?
8. For example, mutilation, branding, bear-baiting, cock fighting ...

Page 79
1. No. They usually wore hats. (He has a hat in his hand.)
2. By ties through holes in each garment.
3. The nobleman is wearing a beard which was unfashionable before 1550. Also breeches became fashionable after 1550.
4. An ordinary working man wore a jerkin, had no ruff and wore a belt around his middle.
5. Primary.
6. True.
7. Velvet cap with a feather, jerkin, doublet, upper stocks (instead of breeches), lower silk hose, girdle, scabbard, robe - a cloak.
8. Rich - his clothes were expensive and he wore gold embroidered cloth and precious stones.
9. (a) worked with a wide band of gold stitching,
   (b) on his leg he wore a garter with the emblem of St George on it.
   (c) a splendid figure of a man.

Page 80
1. Sewing (embroidery) and listening to music.
2. Preparing food.
3. A - upper class, B - lower class.
4. Lower class women.
5. The women in A would have had personal tutors or have been educated at a nunnery. Those in B would have had very little education - they might have learned their letters from the parish priest.
6. See Teachers' Notes.
7. C - lower class, D - upper class.

8. It depends on wealth and dress. Lower class women usually had to do manual work and their clothes were simple in style and made of strong materials. Wealthy women did little manual work. Their clothes were often so complicated that they made manual work difficult and were made of delicate material often richly decorated with embroidery and precious stones.

Page 81
1. Two.
2. Paper was pressed against the metal type which had been coated with ink.
3 - 4. See print.
5. Applying ink to the metal type.
6. Putting the pages of a book together.
   Very young children were employed.
7. Newly printed pages of paper - to dry.
9. See Teachers' Notes.

Page 82
1. Sir Anthony Fitzherbert, 1523.
2. Husbandry, farmwork.
3. Ploughing the soil.
4. Primary. It was published in Tudor times.
5. See passage.
6. Explained in the passage.
   After 1539 it would have been written in English.

Page 83
1. A hospital. St Mary, St Bartholomew and St Thomas.
2. Disabled or sick people. They were considered to be worthy of help unlike the able-bodied poor who were punished.
3. Physicians - theoretical doctors,
   surgeons - practising medical men who carried out operations,
   apothecaries - herbal specialists (pharmacists now).
4. To look after and heal the sick, to house the sick until they were cured and able to work. Those who were fit but did not work would be punished. Thus, there would be few people begging on the streets.
5 - 7. See Teachers' Notes.
9. See Teachers' Notes.

Page 84
1. A contest between two knights on horses trying to unseat each other with lances.
2. The king and nobility.
3. Wealthy.
4. See print.
5. Incognito - in disguise.
6. A lance. It might have broken - there are pieces on the ground.
7. He is the adjudicator or judge.
8. Waiting for his turn at jousting.
9. Yes. See Teachers' Notes.
10. The contestants wore coats-of-arms.
11. Tennis.
12. See Teachers' Notes.
13. Cockpit. Cock-fighting.
14. See Teachers' Notes, e.g. bear-baiting.
15. See Teachers' Notes.

Page 85
1 - 5. See Teachers' Notes.
6. (a) Portside - the left side of a ship when you are facing the nose or the bow of the ship.
   (b) Starboard - the right side of a ship when you are facing the nose of the bow of the ship.
   (c) Keelhauling - punishment in which sailor was dragged by a rope under the keel of a ship from one side to the other.
   (d) Broadside - firing cannon from the side of a vessel.
7 - 9. See Teachers' Notes.

Page 86
1 - 6. See Teacher's Notes.

Page 87
1 - 8. See Teachers' Notes
9.

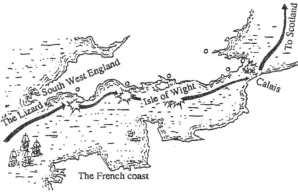

The French coast

Page 88
1 - 6. See Teachers' Notes.

Page 89
Bess of Hardwick - Countess of Shrewsbury.
William Shakespeare - Playwright who built the Globe.
Lady Jane Grey - Nine Days' Queen.
William Cecil - Elizabethan Statesman.
Richard Burbage - Elizabethan actor.
Thomas Wolsey - Built Hampton Court Palace.
Sir Francis Drake - Helped to defeat the Armada.
Desiderius Erasmus - Dutch scholar.
Henry VII - Founder of Tudor Dynasty.

Page 90
1. Henry VII.   2. Richard III.
3. 1485 - 1603.   4. James IV of Scotland, 1553.
5. Leading Minister of Henry VIII.
6. Francis I of France.
7. Defender of the Faith. Yes.
8. Anne Boleyn. He wanted a male heir.
9. No. Elizabeth who became Queen Elizabeth I.
10. The 'Mary Rose'.
11. Anne of Cleves. She was ugly.
12. Holbein.
13. 1529.   14. Somerset and Northumberland.
15. Lady Jane Grey.
16. Mary Tudor. She burnt many Protestants at the stake. 1553 - 1558.
17. 1558.   18. (a) France,   (b) Spain.
19. Secretary to Mary Queen of Scots.
20. Catholic inspired plot to kill Queen Elizabeth and put Mary, Queen of Scots, on the English throne.
21. Mary, Queen of Scots. Elizabeth I signed the death warrant.
22. Philip II.   23. The Spanish Armada.
24. Leader of the Armada.
25. The 'Rebirth of Learning'.
26. The printing press.   27.   Books.
28. Leading Dutch scholar.
29. Someone who paid a fine for NOT attending church

service.
30. The Black Death, a disease carried by fleas on rats that killed may people in Medieval, Tudor and Stuart times.

Page 91
Not available in Tudor times:
calculator, can of coke, computer, fountain pen, telephone, crisps.

Page 92
1 - 7. See Teachers' Notes.
8. A virginals, B viol, C flute, D lute, E harp, F. clavichord, G. tabor (drum), H. shawm, I. trumpet, J. recorder.

Page 93
See Teachers' Notes.

Page 94
See Teachers' Notes.

Page 95

DATE	EVENT
1485	Accession of Henry VII.
1497	John Cabot sails to Newfoundland.
1502	Death of Arthur, Prince of Wales.
1509	Accession of Henry VIII. Marriage with Catherine of Aragon.
1512	Wolsey becomes Henry VIII's Chief Minister.
1520	Henry VIII meets Francis 1 of France at the Field of the Cloth of Gold.
1533	Henry VIII marries Anne Boleyn.
1536 - 9	Dissolution of the monasteries.
1547	Death of Henry VIII.
1554	Mary Tudor marries Philip II of Spain.
1558	Accession of Elizabeth I.
1586	Babington Plot. Trial of Mary, Queen of Scots.
1587	Execution of Mary, Queen of Scots.
1588	Defeat of the Spanish Armada.
1597	New Poor Law Legislation gives relief to the impotent poor. (Renacted 1601).

Page 97
ether - either,   rooste or boyle - roast or boil,
streyner - strainer,   temper them - cool,
damaske water - rosewater,   suger - sugar,
swete butter - fresh (not rancid) butter,
synamon - cinnamon,   gynger - ginger,
serve them forth - serve immediately.

Page 96

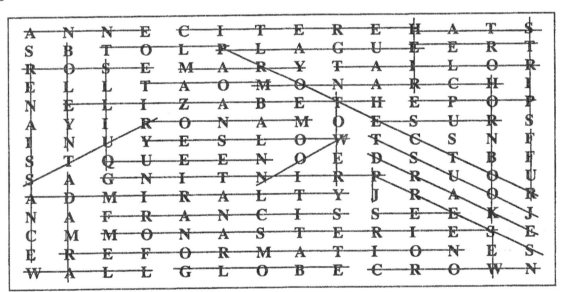

1. Protector
2. Plague
3. Anne Boleyn
4. Monarch
5. Heir
6. Armada
7. Francis Drake
8. Mary Rose
9. Globe
10. Manor
11. Wolsey
12. Strips
13. Rose
14. Heretic
15. Ruff
16. Crown
17. Quills
18. Hornbook
19. Printing press
20. Renaissance
21. Monasteries
22. Joust
23. Admiralty
24. Wall
25. Tower
26. Queen Elizabeth
27. Reformation
28. Plot
29. Pope
30. JP
31. See
32. Moat
33. Tailor
34. Sew
35. Hats
36. Tree
37. Won
38. Ruse
39. Ruts

RECORD SHEET
LIFE IN TUDOR TIMES

Name _____   Age _____

Page	Master Copy		Page	Master Copy	
56	The Tudor Monarchs Genealogical Table		80	Tudor Women	
57	I am King		81	The Printing Press	
58	Primary and Secondary Sources		82	The Boke of Husbandry, 123	
59	School in Tudor Times		83	Medicine in Tudor Times	
60	Henry VIII and his Six Wives		84	Sports and Pastimes	
61	Closing the Monasteries		85	The Tudor Navy	
62	The Boy King - Edward VI		86	The 'Mary Rose'	
63	Mary Tudor - A Catholic Queen		87	The Spanish Armada	
64	The Nine Days' Queen		88	Exploration in Tudor Times	
65	The Virgin Queen - Elizabeth I		89	Famous Tudors	
66	The Death of a Queen		90	Tudor Quiz	
67	Tudor Apprentices		91	Tudor Objects	
68	Work and Workers in Tudor Times		92	William Shakespeare	
69	Life in a Tudor Village		93	The Tudor Legacy	
70	How the Tudors Lived - a Cottage		94	Tudor Documents	
71	A Manor House		94	Letter from Queen Elizabeth I	
72	A Mansion		94	Seals	
73	Tudor Town Life		95	Tudor Time-Line	
74	Tudor London		96	Tudor Puzzles	
75	Tudor Eating Habits		97	Tudor Wordsearch	
76	A Tudor Dictionary Quiz		98	A Tudor Game	
77	The Homeless in Tudor Times		99	Project Ideas	
78	Crime and Punishment		99	Things to Make	
79	Tudor Dress - Men		100	World Map	

MASTER FILES

published by
Domino Books (Wales) Ltd.

AN ESTABLISHED SERIES
prepared by experienced teachers

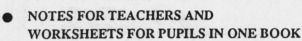

- NOTES FOR TEACHERS AND WORKSHEETS FOR PUPILS IN ONE BOOK

- COMPREHENSIVE NATIONAL CURRICULUM COVERAGE

- THERE IS NO NEED TO BUY ADDITIONAL MATERIAL

- ALL THE MATERIAL IS PHOTOCOPIABLE

- EXCELLENT VALUE

- SAVES YOU TIME AND MONEY

- VISUALLY STIMULATING

- BOOKS SPECIFICALLY DESIGNED FOR THE KEY STAGE YOU TEACH

- FULL OF TEACHING STRATEGIES AND IDEAS

- READY-TO-USE LESSONS

- FLEXIBLE RESOURCES FOR USE BY THE WHOLE CLASS, BY GROUPS OR BY INDIVIDUAL PUPILS

- TRIED AND TESTED MATERIALS

- PHOTOCOPIABLE SHEETS TO USE AS THEY ARE OR TO REDUCE OR ENLARGE

- PHOTOCOPIABLE RECORD SHEETS FOR EACH PUPIL

- NEW TITLES PUBLISHED MONTHLY

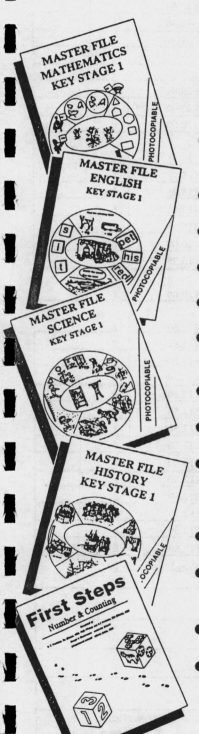

AVAILABLE FROM
Domino Books (Wales) Ltd
P O Box 32, Swansea SA1 1FN
Tel. (01792) 459378 Fax. (01792) 466337
www.dominobooks.co.uk
email: sales@dominobooks.co.uk

ORDER FORM OVERLEAF

MASTER FILE ORDER FORM

KEY STAGE 1 (Age 5 - 7)   KEY STAGE 2 (Age 7 - 11)   KEY STAGE 3 (Age 11 - 14)

Quantity	Title	ISBN	Price	Cost
	KS1 ENGLISH	1 85772 111 X	£20.00	£
	KS1 MATHEMATICS	1 85772 107 1	£20.00	£
	KS1 MENTAL MATHEMATICS	1 85772 154 3	£20.00	£
	KS1 SCIENCE	1 85772 108 X	£20.00	£
	KS1 DEVELOPING ICT SKILLS	1 85772 166 7	£20.00	£
	KS1 HISTORY	1 85772 112 8	£20.00	£
	KS2 ENGLISH	1 85772 085 7	£20.00	£
	KS2 MATHEMATICS	1 85772 086 5	£20.00	£
	KS2 SCIENCE	1 85772 087 3	£20.00	£
	KS2 DEVELOPING ICT SKILLS	1 85772 165 9	£20.00	£
	KS2 ICT DATA AND SPREADSHEETS	1 85772 167 5	£20.00	£
	KS3 ENGLISH	1 85772 127 6	£20.00	£
	KS3 MATHEMATICS	1 85772 126 8	£20.00	£
	KS3 SCIENCE	1 85772 128 4	£20.00	£
	KS3 ICT DATA AND SPREADSHEETS	1 85772 164 0	£20.00	£
HISTORY				
	KS2 Invaders and Settlers, The Celts	1 85772 067 9	£15.95	£
	KS2 Invaders and Settlers, The Romans	1 85772 070 9	£15.95	£
	KS2 Invaders and Settlers, The Vikings	1 85772 069 5	£15.95	£
	KS2 Life in Tudor Times	1 85772 076 8	£15.95	£
	KS2/KS3 Victorian Britain	1 85772 077 6	£15.95	£
	KS2 - KS3 Second World War	1 85772 121 7	£20.00	£
	KS2/KS3 Castles	1 85772 075 X	£15.95	£
TOPICS				
	CHRISTMAS (AGES 5 - 12)	1 85772 065 2	£20.00	£
EARLY YEARS				
	First Steps Basic Activities in the 3Rs	1 85772 130 6	£12.50	£
	First Steps Number and Counting	1 85772 133 0	£12.50	£
	First Steps Beginning to Read	1 85772 138 1	£12.50	£
	First Steps Beginning to Write	1 85772 139 X	£12.50	£
	First Steps Beginning Mental Maths	1 85772 142 X	£12.50	£
	First Steps Mental Maths, 5 - 6 years	1 85772 143 8	£12.50	£
	First Steps Mental Maths, 6 - 7 years	1 85772 146 2	£12.50	£
	First Steps Mental Maths, 7 - 8 years	1 85772 147 0	£12.50	£
	First Steps Mental Maths 8 - 9 years	1 85772 148 9	£12.50	£
	First Steps Developing Literacy Skills 4 - 5 years	1 85772 151 9	£12.50	£
	First Steps Developing Literacy Skills 5- 6 years	1 85772 152 7	£12.50	£
	First Steps Developing Literacy Skills 6 - 7 years	1 85772 153 5	£12.50	£
	Reading and Comprehension 5 - 7 years, Book 1	1 85772 144 6	£12.50	£
	Reading and Comprehension 5 - 7 years, Book 2	1 85772 145 4	£12.50	£
			Total	£

Name/Organisation/School

Address

Post Code   **Tel.**

Contact   **Signature**

Order Number

Date

Available from Blackwells, Bookshop at the Institute of Education, Bedford Way (London), the Consortium (Trowbridge), Foyles Bookshop, Hammicks, Ottakars, Waterstones, Welsh Books Council and all good booksellers or direct from

DOMINO BOOKS (WALES) LTD, P O BOX 32, SWANSEA SA1 1 FN.
Tel. 01792 459378 Fax. 01792 466337
www.dominobooks.co.uk   email: sales@dominobooks.co.uk

All official orders must have an official requisition form attached (schools, educational establishments, LEAs,